MIND YOUR OWN BUSINESS

A Comedy

By James Pattinson

samuelfrench.co.uk

Copyright © 1967 by James Pattinson
All Rights Reserved

MIND YOUR OWN BUSINESS is fully protected under the copyright laws of the British Commonwealth, including Canada, the United States of America, and all other countries of the Copyright Union. All rights, including professional and amateur stage productions, recitation, lecturing, public reading, motion picture, radio broadcasting, television and the rights of translation into foreign languages are strictly reserved.

ISBN 978-0-573-11389-5

www.samuelfrench.co.uk
www.samuelfrench.com

FOR AMATEUR PRODUCTION ENQUIRIES

UNITED KINGDOM AND WORLD
EXCLUDING NORTH AMERICA
plays@samuelfrench.co.uk
020 7255 4302/01

Each title is subject to availability from Samuel French,
depending upon country of performance.

CAUTION: Professional and amateur producers are hereby warned that MIND YOUR OWN BUSINESS is subject to a licensing fee. Publication of this play does not imply availability for performance. Both amateurs and professionals considering a production are strongly advised to apply to the appropriate agent before starting rehearsals, advertising, or booking a theatre. A licensing fee must be paid whether the title is presented for charity or gain and whether or not admission is charged.

The professional rights in this play are controlled by Samuel French Ltd, 24-32 Stephenson Way, London, NW1 2HD.

No one shall make any changes in this title for the purpose of production. No part of this book may be reproduced, stored in a retrieval system, or transmitted in any form, by any means, now known or yet to be invented, including mechanical, electronic, photocopying, recording, videotaping, or otherwise, without the prior written permission of the publisher. No one shall upload this title, or part of this title, to any social media websites.

The right of James Pattinson to be identified as author of this work has been asserted in accordance with Section 77 of the Copyright, Designs and Patents Act 1988.

MIND YOUR OWN BUSINESS

CHARACTERS

ROGER KENTON
VICKIE KENTON
DOUGLAS COULTER
SANDRA WALLACE
ANTONIO DA SILVA
GEORGE LAPWING
STEPHEN BRANDISH
HAZEL GORDON

The action of the play takes place in a small country bungalow which is Kenton's week-end retreat.

ACT ONE   A Summer morning
ACT TWO   The following morning
ACT THREE   The following morning

No character in this play is intended to portray any specific person alive or dead.

ACT I

The scene is a living room in a small country bungalow. There is a window D.R. and underneath it a small table fitted with drawers and an upright chair by the table. On the table is the framed photograph of a school cricket eleven. A door U.R. leads to a bedroom. Against the back wall C. is a drinks cabinet or small cupboard. L. of this a door opens to the entrance hall and this also leads to the second bedroom and the bathroom. D.L. is another door leading to the kitchen and rear exit. Above this door is an armchair pushed up against the wall. There is a sofa C.
ROGER KENTON *is sitting in armchair L. and is studying some typewritten sheets of paper clipped together.*
VICKIE *comes in R. She is dressed for travelling and is carrying a suitcase. She is an attractive woman.*

    KENTON (*in surprise*) Vickie! Where are you going?
    VICKIE (*coldly, putting suitcase down*) I'm going home.
    KENTON Back to the flat! But we only got down here last night.
    VICKIE I am perfectly well aware of that.
    KENTON Then why go back? This was your idea. Let's go down to the bungalow, you said. There are two bedrooms, you said, and it'll be so much nicer entertaining Mr. Da Silva in the country, away from all the other sharks. That is what you said, isn't it?
    VICKIE You don't have to tell me what I did or did not say. My memory is quite as good as yours.
    KENTON Then why, in heaven's name, have you suddenly decided to go back to London?
    VICKIE I have not decided to go back to London.
    KENTON But you just said—
    VICKIE I said I was going home. I am. To Mother.
    KENTON (*getting up*) Oh, lord! Not again. What have I done this time?
    VICKIE You have betrayed me.
    KENTON Betrayed! Oh, come off it.

VICKIE Do you deny it?
KENTON You bet I jolly well deny it. You're barking up the wrong tree, old girl. You're thinking about some other character. Not Roger Kenton, not good old Roger, bless his heart.
VICKIE Really! Then perhaps good old Roger, bless his heart, can explain who this is. *(She takes out a photograph.)*
KENTON Where did you get that?
VICKIE From the pocket of your jacket.
KENTON *(indignantly)* So you go ferreting in my pockets now. There's a trusting wife.
VICKIE It seems I've got good reason to be trusting, doesn't it? Who is this female?
KENTON A business acquaintance.
VICKIE Is that so? *(She reads from photograph.)* 'To Darling Roger with all my love. Sandra.' What sort of business is that?
KENTON You have to maintain good relations these days.
VICKIE Then you can maintain good relations without my help. I'm leaving.
KENTON But you can't do that, Vickie. Not with Da Silva coming. Just think of it—all the way from Chile to find that his hostess has walked out. Think of the evil consequences to international good will.
VICKIE You should have thought of that before you took up with this floozie.
KENTON That is not a floozie. She is a perfectly respectable young business lady.
VICKIE A likely story. You'll be telling me next that she's President of the Board of Trade.
KENTON I shall be telling you no such thing. She's Liberal.
VICKIE That doesn't surprise me in the least.
KENTON Anyway, you can't go now. Da Silva might be offended, and then he might not sign this contract. And if he doesn't sign I'm up the creek.
VICKIE Then you'll just have to paddle down again because I'm going.
(She picks up suitcase and moves towards door U.L.)
KENTON But, Vickie—
(The door-bell rings offstage.)

Oh, lord, that must be Da Silva now. Don't go, Vickie. For Pete's sake stay until he's signed. (VICKIE *hesitates, shrugs and puts down suitcase.* KENTON *goes out U.L.* VICKIE *looks at photograph again, mutters 'Floozie!' and throws the photograph down on table R.* KENTON *comes in U.L. with* COULTER *who is carrying a brief-case.*)

KENTON (*protesting*) I really don't want an encyclopaedia. I don't have any need for one.

COULTER Everyone has need of an encyclopaedia. An encyclopaedia is a fountain of knowledge ever ready to refresh the thirsty. (*He sees* VICKIE.) Good morning, madam. I am sure your husband—

VICKIE (*icily*) He is not my husband.

COULTER Not your—

KENTON Of course I'm your husband. Don't tell such lies to an encyclopaedia man. It's not decent.

COULTER 'Beauty is truth, truth beauty.' Keats. 'Ode on a Grecian Urn.' Volume ten, page 342. The English Poets.

VICKIE I renounce him.

COULTER Keats?

VICKIE My husband.

KENTON Nonsense. I utterly refuse to be renounced.

VICKIE Villain.

COULTER (*sitting down at table R. and taking a mass of papers from brief-case*) Meaning wicked, depraved, capable of crime—

KENTON I am not.

VICKIE You are.

KENTON I am innocent.

VICKIE I shall sue for divorce.

COULTER There is an excellent paragraph on the law of divorce in the legal section in volume eight.

KENTON Why don't you dry up!

COULTER Now, now, sir. Don't lose your temper.

KENTON I am not losing my temper.

VICKIE You're losing your wife. (*She picks up suitcase and goes to door U.L.*) Good-bye.

KENTON (*catching her arm*) Don't go. I'll do anything you want me to. I'll wash up. I'll change my socks. Any-

thing as long as you stay just until Da Silva has been.
VICKIE So that's all I mean to you—a signature on a contract. Well, now we know.
KENTON Of course you mean more to me than that. You mean everything.
VICKIE You can tell that to Sandra.
(She goes out, slamming door. KENTON *winces. The outer door slams. He winces again.)*
KENTON Damn!
COULTER You have my deepest sympathy. It is a bitter thing to lose one's wife.
KENTON Piffle! I haven't lost her. She'll be back. What I may have lost is a contract for a hundred thousand pounds' worth of electrical equipment. This could be a horrible blow to the balance of trade.
COULTER Now that is serious. You have my even deeper sympathy. Is there anything I can do to help?
KENTON Not unless you can impersonate my wife.
COULTER I once played Charley's Aunt— But no, I don't think it would work. Why must you have a wife at this particular time?
KENTON Because a South American named Antonio Da Silva is coming to discuss a business deal.
COULTER The hundred thousand pound contract?
KENTON Exactly. And if I don't have somebody here to cook and all that he's going to have such a rough time of it that'll he'll never agree to sign anything.
COULTER I see. Well, suppose I rushed in with the news that your wife had just been killed in a road accident.
KENTON How the devil would that help?
COULTER He'd be so overcome with sympathy, he'd be ready to sign the contract just to cheer you up. South Americans are very sensitive people.
KENTON H'm. I believe you could have something there. By the way, what's your name?
COULTER Coulter—Douglas Coulter.
(They shake hands.)
KENTON Would you do that, Mr. Coulter?
COULTER I'll do it if you buy an encyclopaedia.
KENTON Done.

COULTER Now perhaps you'll just sign the agreement. (*He produces a printed form.*) Naturally you will want the de luxe edition with the half-leather binding and the real gold lettering.
KENTON How much is it?
COULTER Fifteen volumes. One hundred guineas.
KENTON A hundred guineas! That's a lot of money.
COULTER For such a fountain of knowledge! It would be cheap at ten times the price. (*He indicates place for signature.*) Along the dotted line, if you please.
KENTON I'll sign after I've hooked Da Silva.
COULTER Oh, no. I don't think I can agree to that. I'd much rather you signed now.
KENTON Don't you trust me?
COULTER Trust is a word I never care to use. It can mean such widely different things. I remember a concern called the Antarctic Refrigeration Trust that skinned my poor old Aunt Matilda for every penny she had.
KENTON How much was that?
COULTER Five pounds.
KENTON That wasn't a lot.
COULTER She was a bit low at the time. Now if you'll just put your name on the form everything will be ship-shape and Bristol fashion, as the saying is.
KENTON Oh, well, if I must. Have you a pen?
COULTER Of course.
(*He hands* KENTON *a pen and* KENTON *signs.*)
KENTON There.
COULTER Thank you, sir.
(KENTON *is about to pocket the pen.*)
My pen, if you don't mind. (*He takes it and puts it in his own pocket.*)
KENTON Now you'd better get out before Da Silva arrives.
COULTER (*putting papers back in brief-case*) You will never regret this transaction. An encyclopaedia is a window admitting light to the castle of the mind. It is a silken ladder leading to the stars, a Cunard liner on the ocean of success, a treasure house crammed with the priceless jewels of knowledge and learning. Incidentally, you'll find it very good for pressing trousers as well.

KENTON (*impatiently*) Yes, yes, I'm sure you're right. Good-bye. (*He urges* COULTER *out and shuts the door up* L. *He picks up the* DA SILVA *contract, examines it, shakes his head and puts it in drawer of table. He sits down on sofa.* SANDRA *comes in* U.L. *She is attractive, smartly dressed. She comes up behind* KENTON.)
SANDRA Hello, darling.
KENTON (*starting up*) Sandra! How did you get here?
SANDRA I drove down and walked in. You told me never to bother about ceremony with you.
KENTON I must have been barmy.
SANDRA You haven't forgotten, have you?
KENTON How did you know where to find me?
SANDRA I inquired at your office. They told me.
KENTON They had no business—
SANDRA You are glad to see me, aren't you?
KENTON What? Oh, yes. Yes, of course. When are you going back?
(SANDRA *has been holding her mouth up to be kissed. At this question she looks put out.*)
SANDRA Do you want to get rid of me already?
KENTON No, certainly not. I mean—
SANDRA My suitcase is in the hall. I can stay over the week-end
KENTON Oh, lord!
SANDRA What did you say?
KENTON I said bed and board.
SANDRA You do seem to be acting very strangely. You haven't even kissed me.
KENTON Haven't I?
SANDRA Don't you want to?
KENTON Yes, of course, now that you mention it. (*He kisses her rather perfunctorily.*)
SANDRA Well, that wasn't much, was it?
KENTON I'm not feeling up to much.
SANDRA Are you ill?
KENTON I may be sickening for something. Perhaps it wouldn't be advisable for you to stay. You might catch it.
SANDRA But of course I must stay. Do you think I would leave you alone at a time like this?
KENTON It was too much to hope.

SANDRA I shall nurse you. What are the symptoms?
KENTON I think I've got a fever.
SANDRA You'd better lie down and let me take your temperature. (*She makes him lie down on sofa.*) Have you got a thermometer?
KENTON There's one in the bathroom. But you don't have to bother. I'll survive.
SANDRA I'll get it. Where's the bathroom?
KENTON On the left of the hall. But—
SANDRA Wait here. Don't move. I won't be a second.
    (*She goes out U.L.* KENTON *groans.* SANDRA *comes back with a wall thermometer.*)
SANDRA This is the only one I could find.
KENTON It's the only one there is.
SANDRA You'll have to open your mouth wide. It's a bit large.
KENTON I don't think this is at all necessary.
SANDRA It is necessary. You may have got malaria.
KENTON People don't get malaria in England.
SANDRA Cholera then. Open up.
    (KENTON *opens his mouth and she puts the thermometer in.*)
SANDRA Guess who I saw last Wednesday.
KENTON (*mumbling*) I can't guess anything with a thermometer in my mouth.
SANDRA What did you say, darling?
KENTON (*taking the thermometer out*) I said I can't guess anything with a ruddy great thermometer stuck in my gob.
SANDRA Well, put it back again and don't swear. (*She forces it back in his mouth.*) I saw Priscilla.
KENTON (*taking thermometer out*) Who the devil's Priscilla?
SANDRA Thermometer. (*She presses it back in* KENTON'*s mouth.*) I thought you knew Priscilla. I promised her she could be a bridesmaid when we get married.
KENTON When who get married?
SANDRA You and I, darling. Who else!
KENTON (*taking thermometer out*) But I haven't asked you to marry me.
SANDRA (*pushing thermometer back*) I thought it was understood.

(KENTON *puts a hand over his eyes.*)
Are you feeling worse? Oh dear, I wonder whether it's Yellow Jack. You do look rather yellow.
KENTON (*taking thermometer out of mouth and handing it to her*) What does it say?
SANDRA Heat wave.
KENTON I told you I had a fever.
SANDRA But the temperature's only ninety and falling rapidly. You must be getting better. How do you feel?
KENTON There's a nasty taste in my mouth.
SANDRA You've sucked some of the paint off. Now you may get painter's colic.
(*The door-bell rings.*)
KENTON That's torn it.
SANDRA What's wrong?
KENTON It's Da Silva.
SANDRA Da Silva?
KENTON A South American. I'd better go and let him in.
SANDRA And I'll go to the bathroom and make myself presentable.
KENTON All right, if you feel you must.
(*He opens door U.L.* SANDRA *goes out. He follows. Voices are heard off. Door opens again and* KENTON *comes in with* DA SILVA.)
DA SILVA So nice, so very nice, the English countryside. Delightful.
KENTON (*closing door*) I'm glad you could come, Mr. Da Silva.
DA SILVA Please. No formality. Call me Tonio. And you I will call Dodger.
KENTON Roger.
DA SILVA Ah, so. Roger the lodger. Isn't that what you say?
KENTON Not very often. (*He ushers* DA SILVA *to armchair L.* DA SILVA *sits down.*) Would you like a drink? Whisky, sherry—
DA SILVA No drink, thank you. I am—how do you put it?—on the dust-cart.
KENTON I think you mean water-wagon.
DA SILVA Perhaps. Alcohol clouds the brain, and a man of business cannot afford to have a cloudy brain. He would soon be eaten up by sharks.

KENTON I hope you don't think I'm a shark.
DA SILVA Not at all. You are a typical honest English bull-frog.
KENTON Bulldog.
DA SILVA Dog, frog. It makes no difference.
KENTON It does to me.
DA SILVA And where is Mrs. Kenton? I cannot wait to meet your so beautiful wife.
KENTON What makes you think she's beautiful?
DA SILVA But it goes without saying. All English wives are beautiful, are they not?
KENTON Are they not!
DA SILVA Perhaps she is in the kitchen preparing lunch, eh?
KENTON No. She went out.
DA SILVA But she will be back soon?
KENTON I—er—expect so. If she doesn't have an accident.
DA SILVA Why should she have an accident?
KENTON No reason at all. But accidents do happen. It's all this congestion on the roads.
DA SILVA I understand. Indigestion on the roads. Very bad. And your family?
KENTON Family?
DA SILVA Your children. You have children, of course. I never do business with a man who does not have at least three little ones. A man with a big family—him I trust. It is not so easy for him to run away.
KENTON I see. (*He picks up picture of cricket group from table R.*) These are mine. They're at school just now, of course.
DA SILVA (*taking photograph*) All these?
KENTON Except the one with the beard. He's the umpire.
DA SILVA And the one with the moustache?
KENTON Not him either. He's the head.
DA SILVA And this little one is perhaps the tail. No?
KENTON No. He's the scorer.
DA SILVA (*admiringly*) Eleven boys. What a fortunate man you are. But tell me, how is it that they seem so near to one another in age?
KENTON Three sets of triplets and a couple of odd ones thrown in.
DA SILVA Your wife must be a most remarkable woman.

KENTON Oh, she is. (*He puts picture back on table.*)
(SANDRA *comes in* U.L.)
SANDRA Hullo, there.
DA SILVA (*jumping up*) Mrs. Kenton! How pleased I am to see you. (*He grabs her hand and kisses it.*)
SANDRA But I'm not—
(KENTON *makes frantic signs behind* DA SILVA'*s back.*)
DA SILVA Roger was afraid for your safety.
SANDRA My safety?
DA SILVA Because of the indigestion.
SANDRA I haven't had indigestion. I was just doing my face.
DA SILVA You go out on to the roads to do your face?
SANDRA I haven't been out.
DA SILVA But Roger said—
KENTON I must have made a mistake. I told Mr. Da Silva—
DA SILVA Tonio.
KENTON I told Tonio you'd gone out. But you just went to the bathroom, didn't you?
SANDRA Yes, I did. But—
DA SILVA I do congratulate you, Mrs. Kenton. I should never have supposed it possible.
SANDRA Never have supposed what possible?
DA SILVA You look far too young.
SANDRA Young for what?
KENTON I think Tonio is referring to the boys. (*He picks up the photograph.*) Our children.
SANDRA (*taking photograph*) Are these all ours?
KENTON Except the beard and the moustache.
DA SILVA But surely you know your own children.
SANDRA I tend to lose count. After the first half-dozen it becomes a little difficult.
KENTON Sandra is terribly absent-minded. (*He puts photograph back on table.*) Aren't you, darling?
SANDRA (*sweetly*) Yes, darling. Sometimes I even forget I'm married to you.
DA SILVA (*striking his forehead*) And I forget something too. One moment. (*He goes out* U.L.)
SANDRA What game are you playing?
KENTON For Pete's sake don't tell him you're not my wife. A hundred thousand pounds depends on it.

ACT I   MIND YOUR OWN BUSINESS   15

SANDRA Would you mind awfully much explaining how?
KENTON That madman is here to sign a contract. At least I hope so. But he only trusts men with lots of kids.
SANDRA Oh, does he? And what is this family I've suddenly become a mother to?
KENTON My old school cricket team.
SANDRA How utterly revolting.
KENTON Don't say that. One of those boys is now a rural dean.
SANDRA Mother to a rural dean at my age. What could be more shattering? (*She sits on sofa.*)
KENTON He might have been an archdeacon.
(DA SILVA *comes back with a box of cigars and a bottle of scent.*)
DA SILVA Perfume for the lady. Cigars for the gentleman. (*He hands bottle to* SANDRA *and cigar box to* KENTON.)
SANDRA (*reading label*) Seduction! I wonder whether the dean would approve.
DA SILVA The dean?
KENTON (*hastily*) A private joke. Thank you, Tonio. This is very kind.
DA SILVA Not at all. (*He sits in armchair L.*)
(*The door U.L. opens and* LAPWING, *a burly local farmer, comes in carrying a plucked chicken.*)
LAPWING Brought you the fowl, Mr. Kenton, like your good lady ordered.
KENTON Oh—yes. Thank you, Mr. Lapwing.
LAPWING She said to get it here in good time because you'd got a guest to lunch.
KENTON Yes. Mr. Da Silva.
LAPWING Here it is then. (*He hands the chicken to* KENTON.)
KENTON (*to* SANDRA) Take this to the kitchen, will you?
(*He hands chicken to* SANDRA, *who takes it gingerly.*)
SANDRA Ugh! It feels like a corpse.
KENTON It is a corpse.
(SANDRA *goes to door R.*)
Not that way. That's the bedroom. Through there. (*He points at door D.L.*)
(SANDRA *goes out D.L.*)
DA SILVA She is absent-minded, isn't she?
LAPWING Tasty little bird, that.

KENTON I beg your pardon.
LAPWING Not one of them there broilers. I don't believe in that game.
KENTON Oh, you mean the chicken.
LAPWING What else should I mean?
KENTON Nothing. Of course you mean the chicken. No foul play, ha, ha, ha. (*His laugh is rather forced.*)
LAPWING (*with a perfectly straight face*) Are you feeling all right?
KENTON Oh, yes. Fine.
LAPWING Well, you want to watch it. You business gents, you go at it like steam, and then suddenly, bang, there you are.
KENTON Where?
LAPWING Cracked up. Nervous breakdown. Private nursing home, brain specialists, and bills as long as your arm.
DA SILVA Are you suggesting that Mr. Kenton is unbalanced?
LAPWING I don't know about that. I'm not a doctor. All I'm saying is—watch it.
(SANDRA *comes in* D.L.)
SANDRA What time are you having lunch?
KENTON God knows.
DA SILVA Roast chicken is my favourite dish. And I am sure you are an excellent cook, Mrs. Kenton.
SANDRA Oh, no. I can't cook at all. Roger sees to all that side of the business. Don't you, Roger, darling? (*She sits on sofa.*)
LAPWING Did you say Mrs. Kenton?
DA SILVA Yes.
LAPWING But that's not—
KENTON (*cutting hurriedly in*) It was very good of you to bring the chicken, Mr. Lapwing. You must let me have the bill as soon as possible. Charge what you like, just whatever you like.
(*He is pushing* LAPWING *towards the door* U.L., *but before he gets there it bursts open and* COULTER *comes in very dramatically.*)
COULTER Mr. Kenton. Terrible news. Your wife is dead.
KENTON Not now, Coulter, not now. Things have changed.
DA SILVA What do you mean? How can Mrs. Kenton be dead?
COULTER Killed in an accident on the public highway not five

minutes ago. I witnessed the horrible incident with my own eyes.
LAPWING How did it happen?
COULTER Run over by a road-roller. Came out as flat as a strip of linoleum. Ghastly sight. Not even a decent pattern.
KENTON Coulter, for Pete's sake—
DA SILVA There must be some mistake. Don't you see that Mrs. Kenton is here?
LAPWING That's not Mrs. Kenton.
KENTON It jolly well is.
LAPWING Then who was the lady that ordered the chicken?
KENTON That was the charwoman. I had to give her the sack. She used to steal things.
LAPWING She said she was Mrs. Kenton.
KENTON She was very untruthful. Couldn't believe a word she said. She had illusions of grandeur. (*He turns to* SANDRA.) You are my wife, aren't you, darling?
SANDRA I'm certainly no one else's wife.
DA SILVA Then who has been killed?
KENTON Yes, Coulter, who has been killed? Or is this just your little joke?
COULTER Joke?
KENTON You are quite a joker, aren't you? Always saying things for the sake of a laugh, eh? (*He twists* COULTER'*s arm.*)
COULTER Ow! Yes, that's right. For a laugh.
LAPWING You've got a queer sense of humour.
COULTER Born with it. Kicked my brother out of the pram once to see if he'd bounce.
SANDRA And did he?
COULTER No. Just a dull thud.
KENTON Mr. Coulter sells encyclopaedias. He's a fountain of knowledge. Tell us something, Coulter.
COULTER What do you want me to tell you?
KENTON Oh, anything. Some little snippet of perfectly worthless information.
COULTER Would you like to know about sand-fly fever?
SANDRA That sounds desperately exciting. What is it?
COULTER A short, rarely lethal fever caused by a filter-passing virus which is transmitted by sand-flies, the best known of which is phlebotomus papatasii.

SANDRA How divinely fascinating.
COULTER Shall I go on?
LAPWING Not for me. I don't want to know about fleas' bottoms. I've got pigs to feed.
COULTER Couldn't I interest you in an encyclopaedia?
LAPWING No, you couldn't. Good day. (*He goes out* U.L.)
COULTER Some people just don't want to widen their horizons.
SANDRA Roger dear, don't you think you'd better get on with cooking that chicken? We don't want to disappoint Tonio, do we?
KENTON Are you sure you wouldn't care to have a stab at it?
SANDRA But, darling, you know I can't even boil an egg properly.
KENTON Oh, very well. I suppose I'd better do it. (*He goes out* D.L.)
DA SILVA Mrs. Kenton, you continue to amaze me.
SANDRA In what way?
DA SILVA Making your husband do the cooking. In Chile such a thing would be unimaginable.
SANDRA Oh, Roger loves it. He always wanted to be a chef but his parents wouldn't allow it. I can hardly drag him away from the kitchen.
COULTER How long have you been married, Mrs. Kenton?
SANDRA Donkey's years. I've got eleven children. And one of them's a rural dean.
COULTER Astounding.
SANDRA (*getting up*) Would you like to see the garden, Tonio?
DA SILVA (*also rising*) With so charming a guide, nothing could please me more.
SANDRA We'll explore it together. To tell you the truth, I hardly know it myself.
(*They go out* U.L.)
COULTER She can say that again. (*He goes to drinks cabinet and pours himself a drink. He raises the glass.*) Ladies and gentlemen, I give you the toast of Douglas Coulter. May he go from strength to strength. (*He drinks.*) (KENTON *comes in* D.L. COULTER *quickly shuts cabinet and swings round.* KENTON *is wearing a flowered apron and is carrying a baking-tin with the chicken in it. The chicken has not been drawn and the head and neck are*

hanging over side of tin, the legs sticking out over the opposite edge.)
KENTON Where have the others gone?
COULTER To see the garden. What are you doing with that chicken?
KENTON I'm going to cook it. But it doesn't look altogether right to me. Do you know anything about these matters?
COULTER Not a great deal. But shouldn't that be taken off? *(He points at the head.)*
KENTON I was wondering about that. I had an idea it shouldn't go into the oven just as it is.
COULTER And those legs.
KENTON What about them?
COULTER Well, they don't usually stick out like that, do they? I mean, they're supposed to be folded up or something.
KENTON How can you fold them up?
COULTER Perhaps if I had a go. *(He takes hold of the legs and tries to fold them up. He pushes the chicken off the tin on to the floor.)*
KENTON Now look what you've done.
COULTER *(kneeling on floor)* It might be easier down here. More purchase. *(He grips legs again and tries to bend them. The chicken slides away and he follows it.)*
KENTON That's no use. You're just sweeping the carpet with it.
COULTER *(getting up with chicken)* Well, you hold one end and I'll push the other.
KENTON All right.
(KENTON *puts tin down on sofa and holds the body of the chicken.* COULTER *grips the legs and gives a vigorous push.* KENTON *falls over arm of sofa with chicken on top of him and his behind in the baking tin.)*
You clumsy great idiot. Why did you have to do that?
COULTER Sorry, old man. Don't know my own strength.
KENTON *(getting up)* We're getting nowhere fast at this rate, I must say.
COULTER There's something wrong here, you know.
KENTON Something wrong where?
COULTER *(touching the rear end of chicken)* There.
KENTON What's wrong with it?

COULTER There's a lot of stuff inside there which should be taken out.
KENTON Are you sure about that?
COULTER You bet I'm sure. I saw one being done once. Horribly gruesome operation. You have to cut a hole and put your hand inside, and then you sort of drag it all out. There's some of it looks like rubber tubing and it's slubbery and squodgy.
KENTON What do you mean by slubbery and squodgy?
COULTER Sort of ugh!
KENTON Nasty, eh?
COULTER Very nasty indeed.
KENTON Well, it's got to be done, and as you're the expert you'd better come to the kitchen and give me a hand.
COULTER It's not my job.
KENTON I could repudiate that encyclopaedia.
COULTER That wouldn't be very honest.
KENTON I don't feel very honest.
COULTER Oh, all right. But you'll have to let me stay to lunch.
KENTON Come on then.
(*They go out* D.L. *with chicken and tin.* LAPWING *and* BRANDISH *come in* U.L.)
LAPWING That's funny. They were all in here a few minutes ago. Wonder where they've gone.
BRANDISH Is it all right walking in like this? I mean—
LAPWING Bless you, yes. Mr. Kenton don't stand on ceremony. Come and go as you please here. Lucky you ran into me. Might have lost your way else.
BRANDISH And you say Mr. Da Silva is staying here?
LAPWING I didn't quite catch the name, but there is a foreign gentleman.
BRANDISH A Chilean?
LAPWING He looked warm enough to me.
BRANDISH I mean did he come from Chile?
LAPWING Could have. Well, I'll leave you now. They'll be back soon. (*He goes out* U.L.)
(BRANDISH *examines the room. He looks in table drawer and finds the contract. He gives an exclamation of satisfaction and begins to read.*)
BRANDISH One hundred thousand, eh? Daylight robbery. I can

undercut that. (*He hears somebody coming and quickly replaces contract in drawer.*)

(SANDRA *and* DA SILVA *come in* U.L.)

SANDRA Mr. Brandish!
BRANDISH Well, fancy meeting you here. It's a small world.
DA SILVA Where else would you expect to meet Mrs. Kenton?
BRANDISH Mrs. Kenton! But that's not—
SANDRA (*hurriedly*) I expect Mr. Brandish thought I was still in town.
BRANDISH You bet I did.
SANDRA I decided after all to join my husband. It would hardly have seemed hospitable not to be here to entertain Mr. Da Silva.
BRANDISH So you're Mr. Da Silva?
DA SILVA (*giving a slight bow*) At your service.
BRANDISH I should like to have a talk with you as soon as possible.
DA SILVA Why not now? I am listening.
LAPWING (*glancing at* SANDRA) It's business. Highly confidential.
DA SILVA I'm sure we can trust Mrs. Kenton's discretion.
SANDRA Of course you can. I'm awfully discreet.
BRANDISH Impossible.
SANDRA But I love hearing people talk business. It's the most interesting topic in the world.
BRANDISH Surely there's something in the kitchen that calls for your presence.
SANDRA Only a chicken, and Roger is coping with that. Perhaps you'd like to stay to lunch.
BRANDISH What? Oh, all right. I suppose I might as well pick up a free meal.
SANDRA What a gracious acceptance.
DA SILVA Mrs. Kenton, I wonder if I might use your telephone. I have to make a call to my bankers.
SANDRA Why, certainly. It's in the hall—I think.
DA SILVA If you will excuse me a moment then. (*He goes out* U.L.)
BRANDISH What's going on here? You're not Mrs. Kenton.
SANDRA How observant you are. But I suppose all successful men of finance have to be.
BRANDISH You'd better come clean.
SANDRA Mr. Brandish, are you suggesting that I haven't washed?
BRANDISH You know what I mean. I'm asking what you're up to?

SANDRA And why should I tell you?
BRANDISH If you don't I'll give the game away to Da Silva. I'll tell him who you really are.
SANDRA Oh, well, I suppose you'd find out the truth anyway, a bloodhound like you. The fact of the matter is Roger needs a wife and family to impress Tonio. I'm the wife and there's the family. (*She points at photograph.*)
BRANDISH Good God! Is that Yorkshire or Lancashire?
SANDRA Actually I believe it is St. Crispin's College for the sons of decayed gentlewomen.
BRANDISH And how long have you been a decayed gentlewoman?
SANDRA The rot set in very recently.
BRANDISH And may I ask what happened to the real Mrs. Kenton?
SANDRA The real Mrs.—
BRANDISH Didn't you know there was one?
SANDRA I most certainly did not.
BRANDISH Oh ho! It doesn't look as if your husband has been entirely frank with you, does it? Might be grounds for a divorce there.
SANDRA Very funny. Anyway, I don't imagine you came here to discuss the domestic situation.
BRANDISH And if I know anything about you, you didn't come here to impersonate Mrs. Kenton. I'll bet South East Insulators Ltd. would be interested in making a contract with Da Silva themselves.
SANDRA Not to mention Stephen Brandish and Company.
BRANDISH Well, that clears the air a bit. Now we know where we stand.
SANDRA You won't tell Roger that I'm South East Insulators, will you?
BRANDISH Not as long as you keep quiet about my reasons for being here.
SANDRA It's a deal. Armed neutrality.
BRANDISH There's one good thing—Da Silva hasn't signed yet.
SANDRA How do you know?
BRANDISH The contract's in here. (*He opens table drawer and takes out contract.*) Kenton's price is one hundred thousand.
SANDRA And I suppose you can beat that.
BRANDISH I'm saying nothing about what I can or cannot do. Not to a rival. (*He puts contract back.*)

ACT I MIND YOUR OWN BUSINESS 23

SANDRA I may have an advantage over you.
BRANDISH Your feminine charm? That won't count against hard cash.
SANDRA Not with a hot-blooded Latin American?
BRANDISH Have you no morals?
SANDRA Not in business affairs.
(DA SILVA *comes in* U.L.)
Everything all right?
DA SILVA I don't know. The telephone operator was very odd.
SANDRA In what way?
DA SILVA She told me I was through when I hadn't even begun.
BRANDISH She meant you were connected.
DA SILVA But I wasn't. I was completely detached.
(COULTER *comes in* D.L. *He is wearing a flowered housecoat and is carrying an oil-can.*)
SANDRA What on earth are you doing?
COULTER I'm giving Mr. Kenton a hand in the kitchen.
BRANDISH It's going to be a grand meal.
DA SILVA What is the can for?
COULTER Paraffin. It's an oil-cooker and we've run out of fuel. I'm off to the village to get a fill up.
(*He goes out* U.L.)
BRANDISH If he wanders about the countryside like that he'll get himself shut up. Who is he anyway?
SANDRA His name's Coulter and he sells encyclopaedias. He was going to tell us all about sand-fly fever, but he got cut off.
BRANDISH What a disappointment.
SANDRA I'll bet you didn't know it was caused by phlebotomus papatasii.
BRANDISH I'm not sure I wanted to.
(*Door-bell rings.*)
SANDRA I wonder who that is.
DA SILVA Hadn't you better go and see?
SANDRA I suppose I had. (*She looks at* BRANDISH, *hesitates, then goes out* U.L.)
BRANDISH (*moving up to* DA SILVA *and hissing in his ear*) Don't sign anything.
DA SILVA (*startled*) I beg your pardon?
BRANDISH I said don't sign anything.

DA SILVA That's what I thought you said. But why?
BRANDISH I can bid ten per cent under Kenton's price. Stephen Brandish and Company. (*Hands* DA SILVA *his card.*) There! What do you say?
DA SILVA I shall have to think about it.
BRANDISH That's right. You think about it. Sh! Not a word.
(SANDRA *comes in* U.L. *with* HAZEL, *who is carrying a bucket.*)
HAZEL I hope I'm not being a horrible pest, but— (*She sees the two men.*) Oh, hullo. I'm Hazel Gordon in case you wondered. I'm camping in the next field. Came to scrounge some water.
DA SILVA Do you mean you're living in a tent?
HAZEL Absolutely. There were two of us, but Clare didn't like the earwigs, so she went home.
DA SILVA How unreasonable.
HAZEL She was afraid they'd get in her ears and bore through to the brain. She said she had an uncle who lost his head that way.
BRANDISH It could happen.
HAZEL Not with her. She hasn't got enough brain to be worth boring into.
SANDRA Why didn't she use ear-plugs?
HAZEL I suggested that, but she said what if somebody came to murder her in her sleep. She wouldn't hear them.
BRANDISH She had a point there. It would be very inconvenient not to hear a murderer.
HAZEL I think she was just yellow.
SANDRA You'd better go to the kitchen if you want that bucket filled. You'll find Mr. Kenton in there wrestling with a dead fowl. (*She points.*)
HAZEL Okay. (*She goes out* D.L.)
DA SILVA I can never understand why people go camping.
SANDRA It makes a change. (*She sits in armchair.*)
DA SILVA But think of the discomfort. A hard bed, rain coming through the canvas, slugs crawling over the blankets.
BRANDISH Some people like slugs.
SANDRA And discomfort.
BRANDISH Makes them feel virtuous.

SANDRA   Look at fakirs, lying on beds of nails and all that sort of thing.
DA SILVA   I always avoid looking. It gives me a prickling sensation in the spine.
(LAPWING *comes in* U.L. *with some vegetables.*)
LAPWING   Something to go with the chicken. I'll give you these. (*He hands them to* SANDRA, *who takes them rather reluctantly.*)
SANDRA   How generous of you.
LAPWING   And I'll tell you this—you won't find better vegetables than them anywhere. What you think they had under them?
SANDRA   Earth?
LAPWING   Hog muck. You can't beat hog muck for vegetables. Gives 'em flavour. (*He smacks his lips.*) Well, can't stand here talking. Work to do. (*He goes out* U.L.)
(HAZEL *comes in* D.L. *with bucket of water.*)
HAZEL   I don't think Mr. Kenton is enjoying himself much in there. He's using shocking language.
BRANDISH   You shouldn't have listened.
HAZEL   I couldn't help it.
(KENTON *comes in* D.L. *with a large spoon.*)
KENTON   Isn't that idiot Coulter back yet?
BRANDISH   Haven't seen him.
KENTON   Who are you?
SANDRA   This is Mr. Brandish. He just called.
KENTON   How do you do?
BRANDISH   I am in reasonable health, all things considered. Though I do have this twinge in the left leg.
KENTON   Sciatica.
BRANDISH   Possibly. And then there's a touch of migraine with a jabbing sensation behind the eyeballs. I've got a bit of a rash between the shoulder-blades too.
KENTON   I didn't ask for a complete medical report.
BRANDISH   You asked me how I did. Perhaps you'd like to see it.
KENTON   See what?
BRANDISH   (*removing jacket*) The rash.
KENTON   Not now. I'm in a hurry. Some other time.
BRANDISH   It wouldn't take long.
KENTON   I said not now. Can't you see I'm cooking?

BRANDISH Well, you did ask. (*He puts jacket on again.*)
KENTON Coulter must be drilling for that oil. Lunch is going to be late. (*He notices the vegetables.*) Who brought those?
SANDRA Mr. Lapwing. He said they'd go with the chicken.
KENTON As if I hadn't enough on my plate already.
HAZEL I'll help you if you like, Mr. Kenton. At the price of a meal.
KENTON Are you a good cook?
HAZEL I can make scouse.
KENTON We're not having scouse. But come along. And bring the vegetables.
(HAZEL *leaves bucket on floor, takes vegetables from* SANDRA *and follows* KENTON *out D.L.*)
SANDRA Whatever is scouse?
BRANDISH A nauseating concoction originating in Liverpool.
SANDRA Like a beat group?
BRANDISH Not quite as bad as that.
(COULTER *comes in U.L. with oil-can.*)
DA SILVA Have you got the oil?
COULTER In the can. Funny thing happened though.
SANDRA On the way to the theatre?
COULTER No. In the shop. The man jolly well gaped at me when I asked for a gallon of paraffin.
SANDRA You don't say so.
COULTER I do say so. Pop-eyed, open-mouthed, all that caper. Dash it all, what's so extraordinary about somebody wanting a gallon of paraffin?
SANDRA I expect it was because you were a stranger.
COULTER Ah, no doubt. Some people think all strangers are nut-cases, don't they?
BRANDISH It's the rural mentality.
COULTER Hullo, what's that? (*He points at bucket.*)
BRANDISH It's a pail of water.
COULTER Somebody feeling thirsty?
SANDRA Miss Gordon left it there. She's helping Roger.
(HAZEL *comes in D.L.*)
HAZEL (*to* COULTER) Are you Mr. Coulter?
COULTER That's me.
HAZEL You'd better bring that paraffin. The chef's having kittens.

ACT I   MIND YOUR OWN BUSINESS   27

SANDRA   That must be an interesting experience for him.
COULTER   Coming. (HAZEL *holds the door open and he goes out D.L.*)
SANDRA   Miss Gordon!
HAZEL   Yes, ma'am?
SANDRA   Would you mind terribly much removing that bucket of water?
HAZEL   Okay, dearie. (*She takes bucket and goes out D.L.*)
BRANDISH   We've got enough cooks to spoil the broth now, and that's for certain.
SANDRA   I have a feeling that this is going to be a most exotic meal.
           (LAPWING *comes in* U.L.)
LAPWING   I forgot the parsley. (*He holds out sprig of parsley.*)
SANDRA   What's that for?
LAPWING   Stuffing. You aren't thinking of having roast chicken without stuffing, are you? That wouldn't do at all.
SANDRA   Wouldn't it? (*She takes parsley.*)
LAPWING   Bless you, no. Chicken without stuffing is like roast beef without Yorkshire pudding.
DA SILVA   What is Yorkshire pudding?
LAPWING   (*amazed*) You mean to say you don't know what Yorkshire pudding is?
DA SILVA   I have never heard of it.
LAPWING   Well, how primitive can you get? Foreigners!
BRANDISH   Yorkshire pudding is what you have with roast beef.
SANDRA   Like gravy.
BRANDISH   Only it's not like gravy, of course.
SANDRA   More like a pneumatic cushion really.
LAPWING   Yellow.
BRANDISH   Except when it's burnt.
LAPWING   Then it's black.
SANDRA   It comes up in the oven.
LAPWING   Like a balloon.
BRANDISH   Only sometimes it's flat.
LAPWING   It's not real Yorkshire then.
SANDRA   Just sort of tough and rubbery.
DA SILVA   I'm sorry I asked.
LAPWING   Do you want the parsley?
SANDRA   Oh, yes, thank you. (*She takes it.*) I suppose you

wouldn't care to stay to lunch, Mr. Lapwing?
LAPWING Well, that's very civil of you. There's nothing I like better than a nice bit of roast chicken and all the trimmings.
SANDRA It'll be quite a party.
(There is a muffled explosion off L.)
BRANDISH What was that?
DA SILVA Sabotage in the kitchen.
(The door D.L. bursts open and smoke drifts in. KENTON *comes in carrying the baking-tin with a blackened chicken shrunk to the size of a poussin. Smoke is still rising from the tin.* COULTER *follows with a pan also smoking.* HAZEL *follows him. All have blackened faces and hands.)*
KENTON Done to a turn.

CURTAIN

ACT II

KENTON *and* COULTER *are asleep on the sofa, head to feet with a blanket over them.* KENTON *wakes, groans, sees* COULTER's *feet, grimaces and turns his face away. This hurts his neck and he gives a cry of pain. He shakes the feet to wake* COULTER.

COULTER (*half asleep*) Ten guineas down and twenty-four monthly instalments of four pounds, two and six—
KENTON Wake up, Coulter. You're not selling encyclopaedias now. (*The feet have come near his face again. He pushes them away.*) Faugh!
COULTER (*waking*) Where in hell am I?
KENTON You're not in hell at all. You're on my sofa. You just planted your filthy great foot in my mouth.
COULTER Sorry, old man. I dreamt I was putting it in a door. (*He sits up.*) What time is it?
KENTON Nine o'clock. (*He stands up and groans. His head is on one side.*) Oh, lord, my neck's stuck.
COULTER I know how to cure that. (*He grips* KENTON's *head and gives it a wrench.*)
KENTON Ow! (*His neck is now bent over the other way.*)
COULTER All right now?
KENTON No. It's stuck the other way now.
COULTER I must have done too much to it. Hold on. (*He grips* KENTON's *head again and wrenches it.*)
KENTON Ow!
COULTER How's it this time?
KENTON (*feeling his neck tenderly*) You've twisted the vertebrae.
COULTER That's all right. It's good for them. Keeps the little blighters supple.
KENTON I'd like to keep you supple. Why couldn't you put up at the inn like Brandish?
COULTER Can't afford such luxuries. You wouldn't believe how bad the encyclopaedia business is. Nobody seems to be

thirsting for knowledge any more. They're content to remain a lot of ignorami.
KENTON You mean ignoramuses.
COULTER Mi or muses, it's the same thing. They're not buying encyclopaedias.
(*They have been putting on their shoes.*)
KENTON Too bad. Catch hold of this blanket. (*They fold the blanket.*)
COULTER Where does it go?
KENTON In there. (*He points to door R.*)
(COULTER *takes blanket and opens door R. There is a shriek and he steps hurriedly back and shuts the door.*)
COULTER I forgot she was in there. (*He puts blanket on sofa.*)
(DA SILVA *comes in* U.L. *carrying swimming trunks and towel.*)
DA SILVA (*cheerfully*) Good morning, good morning, good morning.
KENTON (*putting a hand to his head and wincing*) How can you be so disgustingly hearty at the crack of dawn?
DA SILVA I have been for a swim in the river. It's a splendid day. Sun shining, birds singing—
KENTON Don't talk about it. Would you like some breakfast?
DA SILVA I could eat a horse.
KENTON No chance of that. I don't ride. It'll just be pot-luck in the kitchen.
COULTER I'll have corn flakes.
(COULTER *and* DA SILVA *go out* D.L. HAZEL *comes in* U.L. *with a billy-can.*)
KENTON What do you want?
HAZEL I'm on the scrounge again. (*She holds up the can.*) One billy for tea.
KENTON What, no nannies for milk?
HAZEL I don't like goat's milk.
KENTON I'll make a bargain with you. If you go and rustle up some breakfast for Mr. Da Silva, you can have some yourself.
HAZEL Suits me. What about you?
KENTON I never eat breakfast.
HAZEL On a diet or something?

ACT II MIND YOUR OWN BUSINESS 31

KENTON No, I'm not on a diet. I just can't face food at this time in the morning.
HAZEL I can face it any time. (*She goes out* D.L.)
KENTON I'll bet she can at that.
  (SANDRA *comes in* R.)
SANDRA Where's that man Coulter?
KENTON Having breakfast.
SANDRA He's got a nerve.
KENTON Doesn't take much nerve to eat corn flakes.
SANDRA Coming into a lady's bedroom without even knocking.
KENTON I didn't think he got in.
SANDRA Why didn't you stop him?
KENTON We both forgot you were in there.
SANDRA You do have short memories.
KENTON It's what comes of sleeping with somebody else's feet in your mouth. Do you want breakfast?
SANDRA Not at the moment. I want to talk to you.
KENTON What about?
SANDRA Brandish.
KENTON A dull subject.
SANDRA Do you know what he's down here for?
KENTON Haven't the foggiest.
SANDRA He's Stephen Brandish and Company. Does that ring a bell?
KENTON The electrical firm?
SANDRA Exactly.
KENTON You mean he's out to snaffle Da Silva?
SANDRA No less.
KENTON The dirty underhand— I'd never have given him lunch if I'd known.
SANDRA We've got to do something.
KENTON We? What makes you so interested in the matter?
SANDRA (*sweetly*) But darling, you know that anything that affects your welfare interests me.
KENTON Oh! Yes, I suppose so. I don't see what we can do though. Can't kidnap Brandish.
SANDRA Why not?
KENTON (*indignantly*) But it's against the law. It's jolly well illegal. (*He stops and his tone changes.*) How could we do it?

SANDRA We shall need help.
KENTON Coulter?
SANDRA And Lapwing.
KENTON No violence.
SANDRA Of course not.
KENTON I shall have to give a bit of thought to this.
SANDRA You work the old brainbox while I get some breakfast. Do you want anything?
KENTON You can bring me a cup of coffee. Black and strong.
SANDRA All right. (*She goes out* D.L.)
KENTON (*shaking his head*) Some people have no respect for the law. Lapwing, eh? He might do it. He owes me something.
(VICKIE *comes in* U.L.)
VICKIE Roger! I have come back!
KENTON (*swinging round*) Holy mackerel! So you have.
VICKIE Well, I must say you don't seem overjoyed to see a forgiving wife.
KENTON Do you mean to say you're forgiving me?
VICKIE As long as you promise never to see that woman again.
KENTON Oh, gawd!
VICKIE Though of course you don't deserve forgiveness. My mother didn't want me to come back. She said you were a loose liver.
KENTON The old battleaxe. Loose liver indeed! Why, I'm not even a floating kidney.
VICKIE Well, do you promise?
KENTON Promise what?
VICKIE Never to see that Jezebel again.
KENTON What Jezebel would that be?
VICKIE That Sandra woman of course.
KENTON Oh, that one.
VICKIE I'm waiting for an answer.
KENTON Well, er—
VICKIE Roger!
KENTON Yes, dear?
VICKIE Do you promise?
KENTON Oh, yes, I promise.
VICKIE You don't sound very emphatic. (*She sees blanket on sofa.*) What's that blanket doing there?

KENTON   I—er—slept on the sofa.
VICKIE   What on earth for?
KENTON   Just for a change. A change is good for everyone.
VICKIE   I believe there's something funny going on here.
KENTON   You don't look very amused.
VICKIE   I'm not amused. I intend to find out what this is all about. (*She goes to door* R.)
KENTON   Stop!
VICKIE   What's the matter?
KENTON   Don't go in there.
VICKIE   And why not?
KENTON   I haven't made the bed.
VICKIE   Since you slept out here there would hardly be any need to make it, would there?
(*She goes out* R. KENTON *looks nervously from one door to another. He is starting to tiptoe towards door* U.L. *when* VICKIE *comes in again* R. *She is holding a rolled up nightdress in her hand.*)
VICKIE   Roger!
KENTON   (*swinging round*) Oh, hullo.
VICKIE   (*allowing nightdress to unroll and holding it up*) What is this?
KENTON   (*stuttering*) Th-th-that?
VICKIE   Yes, this.
KENTON   D-d-don't you kn-kn-know?
VICKIE   Answer the question and don't stutter.
KENTON   Yes—I mean n-n-no.
VICKIE   Roger!
KENTON   Well, if you really want to know what that is, I'd say it's what's known in the trade as a glamorous nylon nightie. I may be wrong, but that's what it looks like to me.
VICKIE   And whose is it?
KENTON   It's not mine.
VICKIE   You amaze me.
KENTON   Isn't it yours?
VICKIE   It certainly is not.
KENTON   Then I give up.
VICKIE   That woman has been here in my absence. I know it.
KENTON   She hasn't. She hasn't been here in anybody's absence;

she's got one of her own. There's only been Da Silva.
VICKIE You're not surely going to say this nightdress is his.
KENTON It could be. He may have bought it for his wife.
VICKIE Nonsense; it's been worn.
KENTON That's for the customs.
VICKIE Customs?
KENTON If they haven't been worn you have to pay duty.
VICKIE I never heard such an improbable story in all my life.
KENTON You haven't listened very hard.
VICKIE Where is she?
KENTON I tell you there isn't anybody. I swear it. On my bended knees I swear it. (*He kneels down.*)
(SANDRA *comes in D.L. with cup of coffee.*)
SANDRA Here's your coffee, darling. What are you kneeling for?
(KENTON *gets up and* SANDRA *sees* VICKIE.)
Hullo there. Are you a friend of Roger's?
VICKIE (*icily, holding nightdress*) Is this yours?
SANDRA That? Oh, yes. Did I leave it lying about?
VICKIE You did. In my bedroom.
SANDRA Your bedroom? Oh, then you must be Mrs. Kenton. Do take this coffee, Roger.
(*He does so.*)
I'm so glad you've come back, Mrs. Kenton; I was getting awfully tired of being Roger's wife.
(ROGER *splutters coffee.*)
VICKIE You impudent hussy!
SANDRA (*calmly*) Now, Mrs. Kenton, you really shouldn't talk like that to the mother of a rural dean. Though I suppose you'll be taking him over now.
VICKIE Do you mind telling me precisely what you're talking about? Being Roger's wife, for instance.
SANDRA Oh, that was just for Mr. Da Silva's benefit. He only deals with people who have wives and families. Well, one wife and one family actually, if you see what I mean.
VICKIE I'm trying to.
KENTON What was I to do when you'd left me?
VICKIE Hold your tongue.
SANDRA It was all above board. Roger slept out here on the sofa. You can ask Mr. Coulter. He slept on the sofa too.

ACT II MIND YOUR OWN BUSINESS 35

VICKIE Who is Mr. Coulter?
KENTON The encyclopaedia man. You met him before you left. He's having breakfast out there with Mr. Da Silva and Hazel.
VICKIE Hazel? Oh, no. Not another one. This is too much.
KENTON Hazel Gordon. She's camping on Lapwing's farm. Always popping in and out.
SANDRA Luckily, Mr Brandish got a room at the inn.
VICKIE (*faintly*) Mr. Brandish?
KENTON I could hardly have put him up here. You do see that, don't you, dear?
VICKIE (*sarcastically*) Oh, I don't see why not. You haven't anybody in the bath, have you?
SANDRA Perhaps I'd better take that. (*She takes the nightdress from* VICKIE *and goes out* R.)
VICKIE (*collapsing on sofa*) I don't believe it. I simply don't believe it. I've only been away from you twenty-four hours and you've managed to surround yourself with half the rogues and vagabonds in the country.
KENTON Steady on there. All these people are perfectly respectable.
VICKIE It was time I came back.
KENTON You needn't have gone away.
VICKIE I can't think what you see in her.
KENTON In whom?
VICKIE In that hussy.
KENTON But I don't see anything. Don't you understand? She just flung herself at me.
VICKIE You could have stepped aside.
KENTON I was simply being polite.
VICKIE I've never even looked at another man.
KENTON And I should jolly well think not when you've got me to look at.
VICKIE Not that I haven't had the opportunity. Don't think that. Plenty of men would have been only too willing.
KENTON How do you know?
VICKIE I just know, that's all.
KENTON (*indignantly*) Do you mean to tell me that some filthy swine has been making passes at you?

VICKIE Why, Roger, I do believe you're jealous.
KENTON And why shouldn't I be jealous? After all, you are my wife.
VICKIE And you still love me?
KENTON Of course I love you.
VICKIE Kiss me then.
(*They kiss, but the cup in* KENTON's *hand rather gets in the way.*)
KENTON I'd better get rid of this.
VICKIE Perhaps you had.
KENTON (*turning at door* D.L.) For the moment, good-bye. (*He blows her a kiss and goes out.*)
VICKIE (*dreamily*) He loves me.
(DA SILVA *comes in* D.L.)
DA SILVA (*surprised*) Vickie!
VICKIE Tonio!
DA SILVA My angel!
VICKIE Darling!
(*They kiss.*)
DA SILVA But what are you doing in this house?
VICKIE I live here.
DA SILVA With the Kentons?
VICKIE I am Mrs. Kenton.
DA SILVA Then there are two of you?
VICKIE No. The other one is an impostor.
DA SILVA I knew it could not be true. Not a whole cricket team at her age.
VICKIE What are you talking about?
DA SILVA The children.
VICKIE There aren't any children.
DA SILVA Then I have been doubly deceived.
VICKIE And you deceived me. You told me your name was Antonio Rivera.
DA SILVA I was travelling incognito. But you deceived me also. You said you were not married.
VICKIE One never feels married on the shores of the Mediterranean. Besides, I had left Roger.
DA SILVA But you went back to him.
VICKIE I always go back.
DA SILVA How loyal.

ACT II   MIND YOUR OWN BUSINESS   37

VICKIE I believe in loyalty. Quite apart from the fact that I love my husband.
DA SILVA You love him?
VICKIE Naturally.
DA SILVA And me?
VICKIE You are somebody I met in Majorca. You are not really part of my life. You are just an incident.
DA SILVA Nothing but an incident. How deflating.
VICKIE But of course I love you too.
DA SILVA Then I am inflated again.
(*They kiss.* COULTER *comes in* D.L.)
COULTER Good morning, Mrs. K. I see you're in harness again.
VICKIE (*drawing away from* DA SILVA) What are you hanging about for?
COULTER Just giving a hand with the catering and all that.
VICKIE Haven't you got business to attend to?
COULTER Nothing urgent.
VICKIE Shall we go into the garden, Mr. Da Silva? It's becoming rather over-crowded in here.
DA SILVA Certainly, Mrs. Kenton. (*He opens door* U.L. *and they go out.*)
(COULTER *goes to drinks cabinet and is about to help himself to a drink when* KENTON *comes in* D.L.)
KENTON Take your filthy hands off that.
COULTER (*hurriedly replacing bottle*) Just admiring the brand.
KENTON You weren't thinking of snaffling a drink, of course.
COULTER At this time of day! Perish the thought.
KENTON Have you seen my wife?
COULTER Which one?
KENTON The real one, of course.
COULTER I think she's entertaining Mr. Da Silva in the garden.
(HAZEL *comes in* D.L. *with billy-can.*)
HAZEL I'm off now. Thanks for the breakfast.
KENTON Have you washed up?
HAZEL Oh, yes. Do you want any help with lunch?
KENTON I suppose you may as well come if you like.
HAZEL Good-o. See you later. (*She goes out* U.L.)
COULTER That's a helpful child.
KENTON She's a proper little one-man girl guide troop.
(SANDRA *comes in* R.)

SANDRA Have you tackled him?
KENTON I was just going to.
COULTER What's this all about?
KENTON We want you to do a job.
COULTER What kind of job?
SANDRA We want Mr. Brandish got out of the way.
COULTER Are you asking me to do him in?
KENTON Of course not. All we want is to have him off the scene until Da Silva has signed the contract. Brandish is here to undercut me.
COULTER I see. And how do you suggest I should set about removing Brandish?
SANDRA We thought you might get Mr. Lapwing to help. He could shut Brandish in his barn for a day or two.
KENTON Lapwing owes me a favour. I put him on to some good investments in the City.
COULTER But kidnapping is illegal, isn't it?
KENTON You're hard up, aren't you?
COULTER That's true.
SANDRA It'd be worth your while.
COULTER How much?
KENTON Twenty-five quid.
COULTER Fifty.
KENTON All right then.
(LAPWING *comes in* U.L. *with a carton of eggs.*)
LAPWING Brought the eggs.
KENTON And just the man we wanted to see. We've got a job for you.
LAPWING I don't take jobs. I'm self-employed. Eighteen and eight on the insurance card.
KENTON As a favour.
LAPWING Oh, well, that's different. What is it?
KENTON I want you to shut Mr. Brandish in your barn.
LAPWING That's against the law. He'd sue me.
KENTON He'll never know it's your barn if you do it the way I tell you.
LAPWING Go on then. I'm listening.
KENTON In the first place, Brandish is certain to come here this morning because he wants to see Mr. Da Silva. What

I'm going to do is to give him a drink with something in it to make him sleep.
COULTER Have you got something?
KENTON Damn it! No. I hadn't thought of that.
COULTER Bang goes the plan.
SANDRA No, it doesn't. I've got what you need. Wait a second. (*She goes out R.*)
LAPWING There's more in that young lady than meets the eye.
COULTER And if it's anything like the part that does meet the eye, it's good enough for me.
(SANDRA *comes back with a small glass phial.*)
SANDRA (*handing phial to* KENTON) This will do the trick.
KENTON (*taking phial and looking at it doubtfully*) What is it?
SANDRA A harmless little drug. Two or three drops in a glass of wine should be enough. You can slip it in without Brandish noticing.
KENTON That'll be easy enough. (*He pockets the phial.*)
LAPWING What happens after you've put him to sleep?
KENTON You and Coulter come in and cart him off to the barn. He won't see you.
LAPWING What about feeding him?
KENTON You can take him his food after dark.
LAPWING He'll see us when we let him go.
KENTON Not if you put some of the drug in his drink to make him sleep again. You can cart him out and dump him miles away, and when he comes to he'll never know where he's been.
COULTER He'll know he was kidnapped in this house. How are you going to explain that?
KENTON I'll say I left him here asleep. When I came back he'd gone. I thought he just woke up and went home. If I'd known he'd been kidnapped, naturally I'd have told the police.
SANDRA Oh, Roger, you are clever. You'd have made a wonderful criminal.
KENTON Well, Lapwing? Are you game?
LAPWING It's a deal.
(*The door-bell rings.*)
KENTON That's probably Brandish now. Sandra, you'd better go into the bedroom. You other two, go to the kitchen.

(SANDRA *goes out* R. LAPWING *and* COULTER *go out* D.L.)
COULTER (*at door* D.L.) Give us a call when you're ready.
KENTON Righto.
(COULTER *shuts door* D.L. KENTON *goes out* U.L. *and returns a moment later with* BRANDISH.)
BRANDISH Thought I'd just look in as I happened to be passing.
KENTON I had an idea you would. Take a chair.
(BRANDISH *sits in armchair.*)
BRANDISH Is Mr. Da Silva about?
KENTON He's taking a turn in the garden. Did you wish to see him?
BRANDISH (*hurriedly*) Not particularly. I'd have said hullo if he'd been here, but it doesn't matter.
KENTON Would you like a drink?
BRANDISH I don't think so, thank you. Not at this time in the morning.
KENTON Why not? As good now as any other time. I'm going to have one.
BRANDISH You are?
KENTON You bet. Nothing like a shot of alcohol to set the old brain whizzing. Come now. What'll it be?
BRANDISH Well, perhaps a glass of sherry. Though I really shouldn't.
KENTON Of course you should. It'll do you the world of good.
(*He pours drinks with his back to* BRANDISH *and adds a few drops from phial to one glass.*) I'd like to have your opinion of this sherry. I get it direct from the importers.
BRANDISH I can't pretend to be much of a judge.
KENTON Never mind. I never trust connoisseurs anyway. Just tell me what you think of it. (*He hands one glass of sherry to* BRANDISH *and keeps the other.*) Here's to business—mine and yours.
(*They drink.*)
Well?
BRANDISH It's rather dry, isn't it?
KENTON Perhaps you prefer a sweeter variety.
BRANDISH No, not at all. (*He drinks again.*) It has an unusual flavour. Difficult to describe, but quite distinct.
KENTON Something to do with the soil in which the vines are grown, I believe.

ACT II   MIND YOUR OWN BUSINESS   41

BRANDISH No doubt. (*He drinks again and begins to get drowsy.*) Funny. Never known such a thing before. Gone straight to my head.
KENTON   Drink it up. Don't waste it.
BRANDISH (*mumbling*) 'Course. (*He drinks clumsily. His head falls on chest.* KENTON *takes the glass and puts it away.*)
KENTON   Wake up, Brandish. (*He shakes* BRANDISH, *who snores.*) What a poor head for wine. (*He goes to door D.L. and opens it.*) You can come in now.
          (COULTER *and* LAPWING *come in D.L.*)
COULTER   You didn't have any trouble with him then?
KENTON   None at all.
LAPWING   How are we going to get him to the barn? We can't carry him all the way.
COULTER   I've got a car outside. We'll bung him in the back.
          (SANDRA *comes in R.*)
SANDRA   He's certainly flat out, isn't he?
KENTON   Poor fellow drank something that didn't agree with him.
COULTER   Well, we'd better get moving. You take his feet, Mr. Lapwing.
          (LAPWING *and* COULTER *pick* BRANDISH *up.* KENTON *goes to door U.L. and opens it. He shuts it again at once.*)
KENTON   Da Silva's just come in. Take Brandish out the back way. And hurry.
          (KENTON *puts his back to door U.L. and holds it shut.* SANDRA *opens door D.L. and* COULTER *and* LAPWING *carry* BRANDISH *out.* KENTON *moves away from door U.L. and* VICKIE *and* DA SILVA *come in.*)
VICKIE   Were you holding the door?
KENTON   Whatever makes you think that?
VICKIE   Something was holding it.
KENTON   It sticks.
VICKIE   Nonsense. What's been going on in here?
KENTON   Nothing's been going on. I don't know what you mean.
VICKIE   You're up to some mischief. I can see it in your face.
KENTON   What absolute rot. My face is just the same as it always is.
VICKIE   It's got a guilty look, hasn't it, Tonio?
KENTON   Tonio! You've soon become very familiar.

DA SILVA Roger, you have not been honest with me.
KENTON How so?
DA SILVA Which of these two ladies *is* your wife?
KENTON Well, you see—
DA SILVA I see that you have made a fool of me. This is the real Mrs. Kenton, is it not? (*He indicates* VICKIE.)
KENTON Actually, yes.
DA SILVA And this other?
SANDRA I'm Sandra Wallace really.
DA SILVA Why did you tell me Miss Wallace was Mrs. Kenton?
KENTON It seemed a good idea at the time.
DA SILVA I don't know whether I could do business with a man who passes off a single female as his wife.
KENTON Would you have preferred a double female?
SANDRA To say nothing of the cricket team.
KENTON Do you have to bring that up?
SANDRA And the rural dean.
KENTON Look, whose side are you on?
SANDRA I'm on the side of the angels.
VICKIE You won't find many of them about here.
DA SILVA In business affairs trust and fair dealing are essential. How do I know that if I signed a contract you would stick to your side of the bargain?
KENTON But that's a different kettle of fish altogether.
DA SILVA We are not discussing fish. And a man who will cheat in one thing may well cheat in another. Wouldn't you say that was so, Miss Wallace?
SANDRA Oh, undoubtedly. Either a man is honest or he isn't. No half measures.
KENTON What are you trying to do? Queer my pitch?
SANDRA One has to tell the truth.
KENTON One wasn't worrying so much about the truth yesterday, was one?
DA SILVA Miss Wallace was obviously led astray.
VICKIE Roger would lead anyone astray.
KENTON Now don't you start too. If you hadn't run off at the critical moment there wouldn't have been any of this bother.
VICKIE And didn't I have good cause to run off?
KENTON I don't think we need go into that now.

ACT II MIND YOUR OWN BUSINESS 43

VICKIE I'm not surprised that Mr. Da Silva hesitates to have dealings with you after your disgraceful behaviour. He's very shocked, aren't you, Tonio?
DA SILVA Deeply shocked.
KENTON Oh, for Pete's sake! Why don't you go and see about the cooking? Tonio hasn't had a decent meal since he got here.
VICKIE Can't the floozie cook?
SANDRA Who's the floozie?
KENTON (*hastily*) Nobody. Just one of my wife's little jokes. Take no notice.
VICKIE (*going to door* D.L.) What would you like for lunch, Tonio?
DA SILVA (*gallantly*) Anything prepared by those fair hands is bound to be delightful.
KENTON You don't know what you're saying.
VICKIE I think I shall try something really exquisite. Something quite fabulously Grand Hotel. I feel the mood of culinary creation taking possession of me. Ambrosia for six. (*She goes out* D.L.)
KENTON It'll taste like old motor tyres just the same.
SANDRA I've never tasted old motor tyres.
KENTON (*to* DA SILVA) You didn't really mean that about not signing the contract, did you?
DA SILVA H'm! There's a great deal of money involved. I cannot do this thing lightly. And my trust in you has been badly shaken.
KENTON But all that other stuff has got nothing to do with business.
DA SILVA The moral character of a man you are dealing with should always be taken into account.
KENTON Well, my moral character's first rate. Besides, you won't get a lower price wherever you go.
DA SILVA I've already had a lower one.
SANDRA Do you mean Brandish?
DA SILVA Ten per cent lower.
KENTON The snake. After I'd fed him on the fat of the land, too.
SANDRA I thought it was charred chicken.
KENTON I don't think I should rely on him if I were you.
DA SILVA Why not?

KENTON I have a feeling we shan't be seeing Mr. Brandish again. He was called away suddenly.
SANDRA I shouldn't be surprised if the police were after him. He didn't look at all trustworthy to me.
KENTON Men with ears that shape never are. You'd be well advised to sign with me, Tonio. (*He takes contract from drawer.*) Why not do it now, eh?
DA SILVA You may be right. After all, that is what I came for. (*He sits at table and* KENTON *spreads contract in front of him.*) Have you a pen I could use?
KENTON A pen. Oh, of course, a pen. (*He feels in his pockets and then hunts through drawers.*) A place for everything and nothing in its place. Would you believe it? Sandra, have you got a pen?
SANDRA Me? Certainly not. I never carry them.
KENTON Coulter's got one. I'll borrow his. Oh no, I can't do that. He's gone out. There may be one in the kitchen. I won't be a minute. Hold on. (*He goes out D.L.*)
SANDRA Don't sign it.
DA SILVA No?
SANDRA I represent South East Insulators. We can give you better terms.
DA SILVA Are you serious?
SANDRA Never more so. That's what I'm here for.
DA SILVA I didn't realise that. I thought it was for quite different reasons.
SANDRA Don't you think we'd better talk this over?
DA SILVA Perhaps we had. Shall we go into the garden, Miss Wallace?
SANDRA An excellent idea, Mr. Da Silva.
(*They go out U.L. A few seconds later* KENTON *comes in* D.L.)
KENTON Not a pen in the house—Hullo! Where the deuce have they gone? (*He goes to table and looks at contract.*) Not signed either. Now I'll have to catch him again. All for the lack of a ninepenny ball-point. (*He puts contract in drawer.*)
(COULTER *and* LAPWING *come in* U.L. COULTER *is carrying* BRANDISH's *suit.*)
COULTER That's that little job done.

ACT II   MIND YOUR OWN BUSINESS   45

LAPWING He's nicely stowed away now.
KENTON What's the suit for?
COULTER This belongs to Brandish. We took it off him.
KENTON Why did you do that?
LAPWING The barn door isn't all that safe. We had to make sure of him. He won't dare come out in his underpants.
KENTON He'll freeze to death.
LAPWING Not him. It's warm weather and there's plenty of straw. He'll be as snug as a bug.
COULTER In a rug. (*He puts suit on sofa.*)
KENTON What are you going to feed him on?
LAPWING We left him some bottles of beer and some crisps.
COULTER There's mangel-wurzels and chaff too.
LAPWING He was beginning to come round, so we beat it.
COULTER You'd better hurry up and get that contract signed. Can't keep him shut up too long. Somebody might go past the barn and hear him.
LAPWING Not that many people go that way. It's supposed to be haunted.
COULTER Probably will be if Brandish pegs out. A ghost in underpants and a dirty vest.
KENTON I nearly had Da Silva on the hook a moment ago. All I needed was a pen. It's a pity you weren't here.
COULTER Can't be everywhere at once. Where's he now?
KENTON I don't know. He must have gone out with Miss Wallace. I can't think what for.
COULTER I can think of something.
KENTON You two had better clear off now. Da Silva may come back, and it'll be easier to do business without a crowd.
COULTER Very true. Come on, Mr. Lapwing. They should be open now.
(LAPWING *goes out* U.L. COULTER *is about to follow.*)
KENTON Just a minute.
COULTER (*turning*) What is it now?
KENTON Lend me your pen, will you?
COULTER (*taking pen from pocket*) You know, for a top rank business man you're wretchedly ill-equipped. It's no wonder we've got an adverse trade balance. (*He hands pen to* KENTON *and goes out* U.L.)

KENTON Now where the devil is Da Silva?
(VICKIE *comes in* D.L.)
VICKIE You made a fine mess of the kitchen while I was away.
KENTON It was Coulter's fault. He set the stove alight.
VICKIE With his encyclopaedic knowledge I should have thought he could have managed a simple oil-stove. (*She notices the suit.*) Whose is that?
LAPWING Well—er—as a matter of fact it belongs to a Mr. Brandish.
VICKIE Then why is it here?
KENTON He asked me to take it to the cleaners.
VICKIE Can't he do his own dirty work? What's he think you are—an errand boy?
KENTON I shouldn't be at all surprised.
VICKIE (*picking up the jacket*) He's left things in the pockets. (*She feels in a pocket and takes out a notebook.*)
KENTON Don't do that.
VICKIE Why shouldn't I?
KENTON It's a crime to pick pockets.
VICKIE Only when they're on people. Anyway, you can't take a suit to the cleaners with full pockets. (*She opens the notebook.*) Well, well, well!
KENTON What do you mean by well, well, well?
VICKIE (*still reading*) Dear, dear, dear! Who would have believed it!
KENTON Who would have believed what? Don't be so damned intriguing.
VICKIE Your Mr. Brandish must be quite a character.
KENTON He isn't my Mr. Brandish, and you'd better give me that notebook.
(*He reaches for it.* VICKIE *evades him and goes on reading.*)
VICKIE He ought to be more careful, with such incriminating evidence. Oh, dear, dear, dear!
KENTON Give it to me. (*He snatches the notebook from her.*) You should be ashamed. Reading a man's private notebook. (*He opens the book and begins to read.*) Well, well, well!
VICKIE You're at it now.
KENTON Dear, dear, dear! Amaryllis—there's a name for you.

And Marlene. Oh my, what would Mrs. Brandish say if she knew about this!
VICKIE Roger, you're surely not thinking of—
KENTON Of course not. What a man puts in his diary is his business. It's no concern of anyone else. (*He turns another page.*) Anthea too. It's like the roll-call of a musical comedy chorus.
VICKIE Hadn't you better put it back where it came from?
KENTON What, and let the cleaners get hold of it! No, I'll put it in a safe place. (*He stows it in his pocket.*)
(HAZEL *comes in* U.L., *her arms full of bedding, equipment and so on.*)
HAZEL Here I am again.
KENTON What's all that stuff for?
HAZEL It's my bedding. I thought perhaps you'd let me doss down in the kitchen.
KENTON What's wrong with the tent?
HAZEL There isn't one any more. Mr. Lapwing's goats have eaten it. I was only just in time to rescue this lot. Another five minutes and they'd have gobbled up everything.
KENTON What depraved appetites.
HAZEL Well, thanks for the invitation. I'll do as much for you one day. (*She goes out* D.L.)
VICKIE Did I simply imagine it or did a girl really pass through here carrying blankets?
KENTON It's the kind of thing that happens. At this moment it wouldn't surprise me if Father Christmas himself came through that door. (*He points* U.L.)
(*The door* U.L. *opens and* BRANDISH *comes in. He has straw in his hair and is wearing a sack in which holes have been cut for his arms and head.*)
BRANDISH (*wildly*) I've been kidnapped. My clothes have been stolen. I have been exposed to horrible indignities. Call the police. Call Scotland Yard. Call the Vice Squad.
KENTON Calm down, old man.
BRANDISH Calm down, you say! Look at me. Do I look like a person who has any reason to calm down? Would you calm down in my position? Do you realise how this ridiculous garment chafes the skin? Do you realise that

MIND YOUR OWN BUSINESS ACT II

I have been stripped not only of my clothes but of my self-respect? And you stand there and have the effrontery to tell me to calm down. Fooey!
KENTON And fooey to you too. It'll do no good flying off the handle. (*He has manoeuvred himself between* BRANDISH *and the suit. He pushes it off the back of the sofa on to the seat.*)
BRANDISH I'll fly off the handle if I wish to. Who are you to tell me what I may or may not do? Are you my keeper?
KENTON I didn't know you had one.
BRANDISH Bah!
VICKIE Are you Mr. Brandish?
BRANDISH Of course I'm Mr. Brandish. Who do you think I am? Joan of Arc?
VICKIE But if you're Mr. Brandish, your suit is—
KENTON Do sit down, dear. (*He pushes her on to the suit.*)
BRANDISH What were you saying about my suit?
VICKIE Just that—
KENTON (*cutting in*) Just that it was a very nice suit.
BRANDISH Why should she say that? She's never seen it.
KENTON I described it to her. It was such a fine suit I felt I had to tell her about it.
BRANDISH I believe you're cracked.
KENTON Some people might say the same about you. I'm not saying they'd be right, mind you, but if you will go about looking like an advertisement for somebody's pig food—
BRANDISH Confound it! Do you think I like going about like this?
KENTON I don't know. There's no accounting for tastes.
(HAZEL *comes in* D.L.)
HAZEL Hullo! Are you getting ready for a pageant or something?
BRANDISH No, I am not getting ready for a pageant or something. I have lost my suit.
HAZEL You are careless, aren't you?
BRANDISH I am not careless. It was forcibly removed from my person while I was unconscious.
HAZEL Things like that will happen, won't they? But I don't think the suit is far away.
BRANDISH And what do you mean by that?

HAZEL I'd say Mrs. Kenton was sitting on it.
VICKIE (*jumping up*) I—
BRANDISH (*seizing the jacket*) You swine, Kenton. So it was you who took it.
KENTON No, really. I've no idea how it got there.
BRANDISH Lies! All lies! I can see your game now. You wanted to get me out of the way while you put through that deal with Da Silva. But I'll beat you yet. I'll cut the price so small you'll need a microscope to see it.
KENTON You won't get much profit out of that.
BRANDISH Damn the profit. I'll do it at a loss just to beat you, you low-down schemer. You haven't heard the last of this affair, I can tell you. Not by a long chalk. (*He shakes his fist and strides to door U.L.*)
VICKIE Where are you going, Mr. Brandish?
BRANDISH I am going to plan the destruction of all my enemies. Until we meet again. Farewell.
(*He goes out U.L. The others stand looking at one another in silence. The door U.L. opens and* BRANDISH *comes in again with his jacket on. Without a word he strides to the sofa, picks up his trousers and walks out in dignified silence. The others watch him.*)

CURTAIN

ACT III

COULTER and DA SILVA *are asleep on the sofa covered by a blanket.* COULTER's *feet are in* DA SILVA's *face.* DA SILVA *wakes, grimaces, thrusts the feet away and groans. He gets up, his head on one side.*

DA SILVA (*groaning*) Oh!
COULTER (*waking*) What's wrong with you?
DA SILVA I can't straighten my neck.
COULTER Same trouble as Kenton had yesterday. It's sofa neck. Otherwise known as lopsided lughole.
DA SILVA It's very awkward.
COULTER Half a second. I know how to fix it. (*He gets up and wrenches* DA SILVA's *head.*) How's that?
DA SILVA (*head twisted other way*) It's the other way now.
COULTER Ah, reversed sofa neck. One more go. (*He wrenches it again.*) Okay now?
DA SILVA I think so. What a night. I dreamed I was living in a dustbin and somebody kept lifting the lid and shouting: 'You'll have to come out of that. We're putting the bailiffs in.'
COULTER I expect you hadn't paid the rent.
DA SILVA But nobody came to collect it.
COULTER Didn't the dustman call?
DA SILVA Yes, but he said he didn't take live refuse, and went away again.
COULTER The trouble with you is you've been seeing too many kitchen sink plays.
DA SILVA I think it was your feet. They have a very evil smell. (*He is putting on his shoes.*)
COULTER (*also putting on shoes*) That's because they're strong feet. It comes from the encyclopaedia work.
DA SILVA In what way?
COULTER Pounding the old pavements. Shoving 'em in doors. You have to look sharp at that game. Some of those women, they'll cut half your toes off quick as lightning if you

don't watch out. We ought to be paid danger money by rights.
DA SILVA What made you take up that work?
COULTER A fortune-teller said I was destined for a literary career. After that I couldn't very well back out. Couldn't make her a liar, could I?
DA SILVA I suppose not.
COULTER That was a noble gesture of yours, giving up your room to Miss Wallace.
DA SILVA As a gentleman I could hardly do anything else when Mr. and Mrs. Kenton moved back in there. (*He points at door* U.R.)
COULTER Are you going to sign that contract with Kenton?
DA SILVA I have not yet made up my mind what I shall do. I have had some good alternative offers.
COULTER You wouldn't like to buy an encyclopaedia, I suppose?
DA SILVA No, thank you. I should never be able to take it on the air liner. It would be too heavy.
COULTER You could go back by sea.
DA SILVA I don't like ships. They make me throw up my inside.
COULTER Pity.
(HAZEL *comes in* D.L. *with two cups of tea.*)
HAZEL I made some tea for you. It's a lovely day. (*She hands out the tea.*) I think I'll go for a swim. Like to come?
COULTER No, thanks. If human beings had been intended to swim they'd have had fins.
HAZEL I've heard that one before. And if they'd been intended to smoke they'd have had chimneys growing out of their heads. How about you, Mr. Da Silva?
DA SILVA Not this morning. I have had a very rough night.
HAZEL Would you like some porridge?
DA SILVA Not on any account. I have never tasted anything more revolting.
COULTER It was invented by the Scots to keep their knees warm and confound their enemies.
HAZEL I think it's gorgeous. I'm going to eat two bowls of it. (*She goes out* D.L.)
COULTER She'll never be fit to swim if she eats two bowls of porridge. With all that ballast she'll go straight to the bottom.

MIND YOUR OWN BUSINESS

(KENTON *comes in* R.)
KENTON (*breezily, smacking his hands*) Here we are again then. All bright and brisk and ready for another wonderful day.
(*He does some deep breathing exercises.* DA SILVA *puts a hand to his head and groans slightly.*)
Anything wrong, old man?
DA SILVA I am not at my best this morning.
COULTER Mr. Da Silva is suffering from a severe attack of sofa neck.
KENTON Too bad. It goes off though. How about signing that contract, eh?
DA SILVA I shall need to be considerably stronger before I can think about signing anything.
KENTON What you need is a good big bowl of porridge.
(DA SILVA *winces.*)
COULTER He doesn't like porridge.
KENTON Extraordinary. Thought everybody loved it.
DA SILVA I don't have cold knees.
KENTON Does that make a difference?
VICKIE (*off* R.) Roger!
KENTON (*opening door* R.) Yes, dear?
VICKIE Bring me a cup of tea.
KENTON Yes, dear.
VICKIE And don't stew it.
KENTON No, dear.
VICKIE And two lumps.
KENTON Yes, dear. (*He closes the door.*)
COULTER Kenton!
KENTON Yes, dear? I mean—
COULTER I'll probably be leaving today.
KENTON I'll try to bear it.
COULTER You'll settle that little account before I go, of course.
KENTON After the way you bungled things! You'll be lucky.
COULTER It wasn't my fault.
VICKIE (*off*) Roger!
KENTON Yes, dear?
VICKIE Hurry up.
KENTON Yes, dear. (*He goes out* D.L.)
DA SILVA What did you bungle?

COULTER I didn't. It was a pure miscalculation. We ought to have removed the sacks. Finished with that cup?
DA SILVA Yes, thank you.
(COULTER *takes the cup.*)
COULTER I'll take these back to the kitchen.
(*He goes towards door D.L. Before he gets to door* KENTON *comes in with cup of tea. They stop, facing each other.*)
It's a debt of honour.
KENTON I haven't got any honour.
VICKIE (*off*) Roger!
KENTON Coming, dear.
(*He goes out* R. COULTER *goes out* D.L.)
DA SILVA The home life of the English. (*He gives a shrug.*)
(COULTER *comes in* D.L. *just as* KENTON *comes in* R.)
COULTER I'll never trust you again as long as I live.
KENTON That may not be so long. You look pretty sickly to me. (*He picks up the blanket.*) Catch hold.
COULTER (*taking other end of blanket while* DA SILVA *dodges*) I could spill the beans.
KENTON They've already been spilt.
COULTER I won't lend you my pen.
KENTON I'll buy one. (*He takes folded blanket out* R.)
COULTER (*following*) You won't like that. (*He steps through door* R. *and there is a scream. He steps back hurriedly.*) I beg your pardon, Mrs. Kenton. I didn't realise—
DA SILVA You should look where you're going.
COULTER I did look.
(KENTON *comes in* R.)
KENTON You should be ashamed.
COULTER And so should you.
KENTON Walking into my wife's bedroom.
COULTER Refusing to pay me my just reward.
(HAZEL *comes in* D.L. *with bowl of porridge and spoon.*)
HAZEL Scrumptious porridge.
DA SILVA Is that the first helping or the second?
HAZEL Second. I may have another one after this.
COULTER You'll burst.
HAZEL I never have done.
COULTER You must have an elastic stomach.

DA SILVA Have you left any for Mr. Kenton?
HAZEL Oh, yes. There's loads. I made it in the copper.
KENTON You'd better take Miss Wallace a cup of tea.
HAZEL Okay. (*She goes out* D.L.)
COULTER It's not as if I asked for the job. I was only doing you a kindness.
KENTON Kindness is its own reward.
COULTER It was a cut-price operation at that. Some people would have charged ten times as much.
KENTON They wouldn't have been paid either.
(HAZEL *comes in* D.L. *with cup of tea.*)
HAZEL It's rather weak. I had to water it. Anyway, it's wet and warm. (*She goes out* U.L.)
COULTER I should have insisted on cash in advance.
KENTON Why don't you stop moaning?
COULTER Because I have reason to moan. You've abused my hospitality.
KENTON I haven't had your hospitality. You've had mine.
COULTER It's the same thing.
(HAZEL *comes in* U.L.)
DA SILVA Was she awake?
HAZEL Not until I blew in her ear.
DA SILVA You what?
HAZEL I blew in her ear. It always wakes them up. Something to do with vibration of the ear-drum. Well, I'd better finish my porridge. (*She goes out* D.L.)
DA SILVA I think I'll take a stroll in the garden to clear my head. (*He goes out* U.L.)
COULTER I hardly expected this kind of treatment.
KENTON I wish you'd shut up.
COULTER If you ask me, it's not surprising that your wife keeps leaving you. What I can't understand is why she married you in the first place.
VICKIE (*coming in* R.) I've often wondered myself.
KENTON Nonsense. You married me because you thought I was the noblest, most handsome man in the world.
VICKIE What can have given me such a ridiculous idea? Where's Tonio?
KENTON He's taking his constitutional in the garden.
VICKIE I think I'll join him. (*She goes out* U.L.)

KENTON I wonder what Brandish is doing?
COULTER Ringing his solicitors, I should think.
KENTON Some people have no sense of humour. You'd have thought he'd have seen the funny side of it.
COULTER Perhaps things don't look so funny from the inside of a hessian nightshirt.
(HAZEL *comes in D.L. carrying swimsuit and towel.*)
HAZEL I'm off for a swim.
COULTER You ought to let that breakfast digest first.
HAZEL Oh, it has. I've got a very rapid digestion.
KENTON Well, don't get drowned.
HAZEL Not me. I'm going to swim the Channel next year.
COULTER Why?
HAZEL I bet Clare I would. She'd like to do it too, but she's afraid of the jelly-fish.
COULTER Do you think you'll manage it?
HAZEL Oh, yes. Once you've made a start there's nothing to it. You just keep on swimming until you reach the other side. 'Bye for now. (*She goes out* U.L.)
KENTON I'd never realised it was quite so easy to swim the English Channel. I wonder why they make such a fuss about it.
(SANDRA *comes in* U.L.)
SANDRA Good morning.
KENTON Want any breakfast?
SANDRA No, thank you. I'll hold out until lunch. Are the others all up?
KENTON Up and out.
SANDRA Da Silva?
KENTON Walking in the garden.
SANDRA He hasn't signed anything?
KENTON Not a thing.
SANDRA That's all right then.
KENTON What do you mean, that's all right? I want him to sign.
SANDRA Yes, of course. I meant it was a good thing that Brandish hadn't caught him.
COULTER There's still time for that. I'll wager Brandish is just burning to get that contract after what he's been through.
SANDRA Out of revenge?

COULTER Exactly.
(LAPWING *comes in U.L. carrying a milk-can.*)
LAPWING 'Morning all. I brought the milk.
KENTON I didn't order any milk.
LAPWING It's a gift. Goat's milk. Pulled with my own two hands this very morning.
SANDRA Goat's milk! Ugh!
LAPWING Best you can have. Full of butter-fat and vitamins.
COULTER To say nothing of Hazel Gordon's tent.
LAPWING I'll put it in the kitchen. (*He goes out D.L.*)
KENTON This house might as well be a public highway. People walk in and out just as they please.
(LAPWING *comes back.*)
LAPWING I saw Mr. Brandish.
COULTER What was he doing?
LAPWING Grinding his teeth.
COULTER Getting ready to bite Mr. Kenton, I expect. What a headline for the Sunday dreadfuls: 'Outbreak of cannibalism in the Home Counties!' 'Gruesome death of well-known business man!'
KENTON I suppose you think that's funny.
COULTER If Brandish made a meal of you I'd crease myself. After the way you've treated me.
SANDRA How has he treated you?
COULTER Refused to pay me.
SANDRA Roger never could be trusted.
KENTON Balderdash.
LAPWING He said to tell you you'd be seeing him very soon.
COULTER Well, that's something to look forward to.
SANDRA I don't think I'll wait for Mr. Brandish. I'm allergic to disgruntled citizens at this hour of the day. (*She goes out U.L.*)
LAPWING I'm off too. I've got the pigs to feed. (*He goes out U.L.*)
KENTON (*to* COULTER) Aren't you beating it too?
COULTER Not me. I want to see Brandish sinking his fangs into your flesh.
KENTON You may be disappointed. I may bite him instead.
COULTER You should have eaten your porridge if you're that hungry. Personally, I wouldn't bite him with somebody else's false teeth.

(BRANDISH *comes in* U.L.)
KENTON Why, if it isn't Mr. Brandish. Clothed and in his right mind. Well, clothed at any rate.
BRANDISH Kenton, I'm going to sue you.
KENTON That'll be nice. I've never been sued before.
BRANDISH You won't find it so amusing when you have to pay whacking great damages.
KENTON Shouldn't you say swingeing damages?
BRANDISH Never mind what I should say. I'm going to squeeze you till the pips squeak.
COULTER Do you mind if I listen in?
BRANDISH You keep your nose out of this.
COULTER Certainly.
KENTON Do you really mean this about suing me?
BRANDISH You can bet your boots I mean it. I just dropped in to tell you, so that you can enjoy thinking about it. I shouldn't be surprised if you went to gaol over this.
COULTER Ten years in Wormwood Scrubs. Skilly in the morning and the cells at night.
BRANDISH I told you to keep your nose out. This is a discussion between gentlemen.
COULTER I'd never have guessed.
BRANDISH I'm getting in touch with my legal adviser straight away.
KENTON I'll give you some legal advice for nothing. Drop the whole idea.
BRANDISH Oh yes, you'd like that, wouldn't you? But not on your life. You're going to squirm like a worm on a hook.
KENTON Haven't you forgotten something?
BRANDISH Forgotten something! What are you getting at?
KENTON Amaryllis, Marlene, Anthea—
BRANDISH Good God! (*He slaps a hand to his pocket.*)
KENTON (*taking out the notebook*) Is this what you're looking for?
BRANDISH You rotten thief! You picked my pocket as well.
KENTON Just insurance.
COULTER A discussion between gentlemen! My, my!
BRANDISH Give me that notebook.
KENTON Not until you sign this. (*He takes a sheet of paper from his pocket.*)

BRANDISH What's that?
KENTON Merely a statement clearing me of any involvement in your recent unfortunate experience.
BRANDISH I'll be damned if I sign that.
KENTON You'll be damned if you don't. I'll give this notebook to your wife.
COULTER What's in the notebook?
KENTON Some rather interesting information. Well, Brandish, are you going to sign?
BRANDISH You'll pay for this some day.
KENTON I can wait.
BRANDISH Give me the paper then. (*He takes paper from* KENTON *and signs it with his own pen.*) There.
KENTON I knew you'd be reasonable. (*He takes the paper and hands notebook to* BRANDISH.)
BRANDISH (*pocketing notebook*) I'll beat you out of that contract with Da Silva now if it's the last thing I do. (*He goes out* U.L.)
COULTER You're not very squeamish about ways and means, are you?
KENTON You can't afford to be in this trade. If you don't cut somebody else's throat, they'll cut yours.
(COULTER *moves to door* D.L.)
Where are you going?
COULTER I'm going to get some breakfast. (*He goes out* D.L.)
(DA SILVA *comes in* U.L.)
KENTON Have you seen my wife?
DA SILVA I left her pondering in the garden.
KENTON She doesn't have to do that. We have a jobbing gardener for the rough work.
DA SILVA I think she has a problem.
KENTON Who hasn't? (*He takes contract from drawer.*) Suppose you sign this contract now, eh?
DA SILVA If you wish. Perhaps I owe you that much. You have a pen?
KENTON Damn! Wait here a second. Don't move an inch. (*He goes to door* D.L. *opens it and shouts.*) Coulter!
COULTER (*appearing in doorway with slice of toast in hand*) Did you want something?
KENTON Lend me your pen, will you?

COULTER Not on your life. I wouldn't lend you a shoulder to weep on.
KENTON I don't want a shoulder to weep on. All I want is a pen.
COULTER The answer's still no.
KENTON Ah, come on. Don't be so unreasonable.
COULTER I'm not being unreasonable. I'm just paying you back in your own coin.
KENTON You mean you absolutely refuse to let me have the loan of a measly ball-point for just ten seconds?
COULTER Not even for half a second.
KENTON Is that your last word?
COULTER Not at all.
KENTON Now what do you mean by that?
COULTER I mean I'll sell it to you.
KENTON That's all right then. How much do you want? Will a shilling be all right?
COULTER No, it will not. This pen will cost you precisely fifty pounds.
KENTON Fifty pounds! You're out of your mind.
DA SILVA Mr. Coulter puts a high price on his pen. Is it made of gold?
COULTER It's a very valuable pen—to Mr. Kenton. Isn't it, Roger? You wouldn't want the fish to slip off the hook again, would you?
DA SILVA Fish?
KENTON A figure of speech.
COULTER Come along, Kenton; write me out a cheque for fifty pounds and you've got your contract.
KENTON Damn you, Coulter. (*He takes a cheque-book from drawer.*)
COULTER An agreement between gentlemen, isn't that what you'd call it?
KENTON Give me the pen.
(COULTER *hands him the pen and he begins to write the cheque.*)
COULTER Make it out to Douglas Montgomery Coulter, if you please.
KENTON Montgomery! What next! (*He hands cheque to* COULTER *and absentmindedly gives him back the pen too.*)
COULTER (*putting pen and cheque in pocket*) Thanks, old boy.

I knew you couldn't be as dishonest as you look. (*He goes out D.L.*)
KENTON (*to* DA SILVA) Now we can get that contract signed. Fifty pounds! The rogue!
DA SILVA If you'll give me the pen.
KENTON The pen! Why, that blighter took it away again. Don't move. Stay right here. (*He rushes out D.L.*) Coulter! Coulter!
(VICKIE *comes in* U.L.)
VICKIE Oh, good. You're alone.
DA SILVA Roger will be back in a moment.
VICKIE Come out here then. (*They go out* U.L.)
(KENTON *comes in* D.L. *with pen.*)
KENTON I've got it. (*He sees that* DA SILVA *has gone.*) Oh lord, now he's gone. There must be a hoodoo on this contract. (*He picks it up.*)
(SANDRA *comes in* U.L.)
SANDRA Hullo. Are you still trying to get a signature on that thing?
KENTON It's my life's work. Have you seen Da Silva?
SANDRA No. I've been in my room.
KENTON (*putting contract in drawer*) He's slipped through my fingers again. Just when I thought I had him. (*He goes to door* U.L.)
SANDRA Where are you going?
KENTON I'm going to look for him.
SANDRA I'll come and help you. I want to see Mr. Da Silva too. (*They go out* U.L. COULTER *comes in* D.L. *He goes to drinks cabinet and helps himself to a drink. He takes the cheque from his pocket and kisses it.*)
COULTER Fifty of the best. I hope it doesn't bounce.
(LAPWING *comes in* U.L.)
LAPWING Have you seen Mr. Kenton?
COULTER Many times.
LAPWING Do you know where he is?
COULTER At this moment, no. The last time I saw him he was in the pen market.
LAPWING Pen market?
COULTER Just between you and me, Mr. Lapwing, I think Kenton's got a thing about pens. He pays vast sums for them.

LAPWING Get away.
COULTER It's the truth. He paid me fifty pounds for an ordinary half-used ball-point that only cost me ninepence when new. Here's the cheque.
LAPWING Well, blow me down! (*He takes several pens from an inner pocket.*) Do you think he'd buy these?
COULTER I shouldn't be at all surprised.
LAPWING Fifty quid a time. That's real money.
COULTER It certainly is.
(VICKIE *comes in* U.L.)
LAPWING Hullo. You came back then.
VICKIE (*coldly*) I beg your pardon, Mr. Lapwing.
LAPWING So you ought. I wonder you had the nerve to show your face in here again.
VICKIE What are you talking about?
LAPWING Telling me you were Mrs. Kenton. That was a good one.
VICKIE Mr. Lapwing, have you been drinking?
LAPWING Drinking! Not me. Though I wouldn't be at all surprised if you'd had one or two. (*He digs her in the ribs.*) Eh, Mrs. Kenton?
VICKIE How dare you! Mr. Coulter, are you going to stand by and watch me being insulted by this uncouth goatherd?
COULTER Would you rather I left the room?
VICKIE (*stamping her foot*) Oh!
LAPWING Aren't you afraid they'll hand you over to the coppers for pinching things? If I was you I'd get out while the going's good.
VICKIE Really, this is too much. Mr. Lapwing, I demand an immediate apology.
LAPWING An apology, is it? That's another good one. A light-fingered charwoman demanding an apology.
VICKIE (*gasping*) Light-fingered charwoman!
LAPWING How you thought you could get away with it, I don't know. But I've got to hand it to you: you carry it off well. Quite the lady. (*He nudges her again.*)
VICKIE Mr. Lapwing, leave my house this instant.
LAPWING Well, you do keep it up and no mistake. (*He puts an arm round her.*) Come on now, why don't you admit that you're no more Mrs. Kenton than I am?

VICKIE (*struggling*) Let me go, you—
LAPWING Give us a kiss first.
(*He tries to kiss her.* VICKIE *kicks his shins and he releases her. She runs out R.*)
COULTER You're quite the ladies' man, aren't you?
LAPWING (*rubbing his shins*) She's a Tartar, she is.
COULTER Aren't you afraid she'll tell Mr. Kenton about you?
LAPWING What if she does?
COULTER He might cut up rough if he hears you've treated his wife like that.
LAPWING But she isn't his wife. She's just a charwoman who steals things. He said so.
COULTER I'm afraid you're out of date. That was a story Kenton made up when he wanted to make Da Silva think Miss Wallace was his wife.
LAPWING You mean to say that one really was Mrs. Kenton?
COULTER None other.
LAPWING Oh, my gawd!
(KENTON *comes in* U.L.)
KENTON I can't find Da Silva anywhere.
COULTER Perhaps he's gone into hiding.
KENTON Why should he do that?
COULTER Latin Americans have strange customs.
LAPWING (*taking pens from pocket*) How much will you give me for these, Mr. Kenton?
KENTON Why the devil should I give you anything for those?
LAPWING You can have the lot for two hundred quid.
KENTON Have you been standing out in the sun?
LAPWING Mr. Coulter said you were buying up old pens.
KENTON Mr. Coulter is a very funny man.
LAPWING I'll take a hundred.
KENTON Put them away and get out of here. I haven't time to play games with you.
LAPWING Fifty quid and a pencil thrown in.
KENTON Can't you understand I don't want any pens? I have the only pen I need. Now get out of this house before I throw you out.
LAPWING All right. Don't get vicious. I'm going. (*He goes out* U.L.)
KENTON I wonder whether he sneaked into the kitchen.

COULTER Lapwing?
KENTON No. Da Silva.
COULTER Why don't you look?
KENTON I will. (*He goes out D.L.*)
(VICKIE *comes in R. carrying a suitcase.*)
VICKIE Has that madman gone?
COULTER Which one?
VICKIE That agricultural Casanova.
COULTER Yes, he's gone.
VICKIE He ought to be locked up in a padded pigsty. (*She goes out U.L.*)
COULTER What a restless family. Must have ants in the pants. (KENTON *comes in D.L.*)
KENTON He isn't in there.
COULTER Maybe he slipped down the sink.
KENTON He can't have. There's a strainer.
COULTER Did you look in the oven?
KENTON What would he be doing in there?
COULTER Getting warm.
KENTON It isn't big enough.
COULTER He may have curled up small.
KENTON The fact of the matter is, fate is against me. I am the plaything of the gods.
COULTER A clockwork toy with a broken spring.
(LAPWING *comes in U.L. with a large blue pencil.*)
LAPWING You can have this one for five pounds.
KENTON (*furiously*) I wouldn't give you five pence for it. Get out and stay out.
LAPWING I was only trying to do you a good turn.
KENTON I don't want any good turns done me.
COULTER His spring is broken.
LAPWING You won't get a better one.
KENTON I don't want a better one. Beat it before I beat you.
LAPWING Some people don't know their own minds. (*He goes out U.L.*)
KENTON Why did you have to put that idea into his head?
COULTER I didn't think he'd take it seriously.
KENTON Lapwing takes everything seriously. Even goats.
(HAZEL *comes in U.L. carrying towel and wet swimsuit, and a letter.*)

HAZEL Here's a letter for you, Mr. Kenton.
KENTON Did the postman ask you to bring it?
HAZEL Oh, no. It's from Mrs. Kenton. She told me to give it to you. (*She hands letter to* KENTON.)
KENTON Why the deuce should Vickie write letters to me? I was speaking to her not half an hour ago.
COULTER Why not open it and see what she says?
(KENTON *opens letter and begins to read*.)
KENTON 'My dearest Roger, When you read this I shall already be on my way to London Airport with Antonio. I have come to the realisation that he is the man I really love, and I cannot live without him. Do not attempt to follow me; I shall never return. The die is cast, my bridges are burnt and I have crossed the Hellespont.'
COULTER Hellespont?
KENTON She means the Rubicon. She never was any good at geography.
HAZEL It was Byron who swam the Hellespont.
COULTER And Leander.
HAZEL What else does she say?
KENTON (*reading*) 'Your ever loving wife, Victoria. P.S. There is a rice pudding in the oven.' Rice pudding!
HAZEL Don't you like rice pudding?
KENTON Where was Mrs. Kenton when she gave you this?
HAZEL She was getting into a car with Mr. Da Silva.
KENTON Betrayed by the woman I was once proud to call my wife! Is there no justice?
COULTER What will you do?
KENTON I shall go after her, of course. You don't imagine I'm going to take this lying down, do you? (*He goes to table and hunts in drawer*.)
COULTER But it's no use. She said she wouldn't come back.
KENTON (*taking out contract*) Who's talking about her coming back? It's Da Silva I want. He hasn't signed the contract. (*He rushes to door* U.L. *and turns*.) If anybody asks for me, I'm on my way to London Airport. (*He goes out* U.L.)
COULTER There goes a devoted husband. Devoted to L.S.D.
HAZEL I don't think he'll catch them. They had a Jaguar.
(SANDRA *comes in* U.L.)

ACT III MIND YOUR OWN BUSINESS 65

SANDRA Have you seen Mr. Da Silva?
HAZEL He's on his way to London Airport with Mrs. Kenton.
COULTER And Mr. Kenton is in hot pursuit, armed with a blank contract and a fifty-pound ball-point pen.
SANDRA Good-bye. (*She goes to door* U.L.)
COULTER Won't you stay to lunch?
HAZEL There's rice pudding.
SANDRA I have no time for luxuries. I must go at once.
HAZEL Where to?
SANDRA London Airport. Hot foot. (*She goes out* U.L.)
COULTER And hell-for-leather.
HAZEL What's biting everybody?
COULTER It must be the migrating season.
(BRANDISH *comes in* U.L.)
BRANDISH Where's that woman off to?
COULTER What woman?
BRANDISH Miss Wallace. I just saw her hopping into a car.
COULTER Maybe she's practising for the high jump.
BRANDISH I've got to see Da Silva.
COULTER Have you brought a telescope?
BRANDISH Where is he? I demand to be told where he is. (*He strides to door* D.L. *and opens it.*)
COULTER You won't find him in there.
(BRANDISH *crosses to door* R. *and opens it.*)
Where are your manners, Mr. Brandish? That's a lady's bedroom. At least, that's her story.
(BRANDISH *closes door.*)
HAZEL But the lady has gone away with Mr. Da Silva.
BRANDISH What's that you say? Gone with Da Silva! Where?
COULTER Eventually to the west coast of South America. Initially to London Airport.
HAZEL And Mr. Kenton is following them, and Miss Wallace is following him.
BRANDISH (*rushing to door* U.L.) Good-bye.
HAZEL Are you going to London Airport too?
BRANDISH I am. (*He goes out* U.L.)
COULTER If only I'd invested my capital in South American Airways.
HAZEL Have you any capital?
COULTER Fifty pounds.

E

HAZEL Would you like to buy me a new tent?
COULTER I'm not irresistibly drawn to the idea. (*He moves towards door D.L.*)
HAZEL What are you going to do now?
COULTER I'm going to see how that rice pudding is coming along. Do you want some?
HAZEL I adore rice pudding. Do you think I could have treacle with it?
COULTER I don't see why not. (*They go out D.L.*)
LAPWING (*excitedly, off U.L.*) Mr. Kenton! Mr. Kenton!
(LAPWING *bursts in U.L. carrying an enormous pencil. He stops, looks round the empty room in surprise. He scratches his head with the pencil in bewilderment.*)

CURTAIN

PRODUCTION NOTE

Though all the parts in the play are important and provide ample opportunity for good acting, the action undoubtedly revolves on Roger Kenton. Kenton, who should preferably be in the middle thirties, has one object only—getting Da Silva's signature. He is willing to adopt almost any measure to attain this end, and it is the continual frustration of his endeavours and his mounting desperation that provide much of the comedy.

Vickie is somewhat younger than her husband and should be elegant and attractive. She is impulsive and volatile, quickly changing from one mood to another and quite ready to fall into Da Silva's arms a moment after having made up her quarrel with Roger.

Coulter may be almost any age from twenty to forty, though about twenty-five would be ideal. He is a happy-go-lucky man, not weighed down with morals if they stand in the way of making some quick money.

Sandra, like Vickie, is young and attractive, but she has a tough business streak. She is completely self-assured and is quite capable of holding her own with the men in any slightly illegal transaction.

Da Silva is about forty and is the average Englishman's idea of a typical Latin American, mercurial and amorous and slightly confounded by the language. He accepts as a matter of course the strange goings-on in Kenton's house, no doubt regarding them as the normal way of life of the eccentric English.

Lapwing is a middle-aged, heavy man, apparently slow-witted, but shrewd enough to see where his own advantage lies. He may speak with a rural accent, but this need not be strongly marked or regionally identifiable.

Brandish is about fifty. He is a blustering, overbearing type of man, very much concerned for his dignity, and this makes all the more amusing his undignified appearance at the end of Act II.

Hazel is a teenager. She should give the impression that she is thoroughly enjoying herself and is not greatly bothered by anything that occurs. She observes the peculiar actions of the adults with a tolerant if rather amused eye.

PRODUCTION NOTE

The play calls for a light touch in production, and though clarity should never be sacrificed to speed at all costs, the scenes should nevertheless not be allowed to drag. The 'business' is merely indicated; it can of course be elaborated according to the ideas of individual producers.

JAMES PATTINSON

PROPERTY LIST

ACT ONE
Set:
Framed photograph of cricket team
    on table
Contract in table drawer
Bottles of wine, glasses, etc. in cabinet

Offstage L.
KENTON
    Baking-tin for chicken
    Large spoon
    Burnt chicken
    Apron
COULTER
    Flowered house-coat
    Oil-can
SANDRA
    Thermometer
DA SILVA
    Box of cigars
    Bottle of scent
LAPWING
    Plucked chicken
    Vegetables and parsley
HAZEL
    Bucket

ACT TWO
Blanket on sofa
KENTON's and COULTER's shoes on floor

Offstage L:
DA SILVA
    Swimming trunks and towel
HAZEL
    Billy-can
    Bedding and camping gear
SANDRA
    Cup of coffee
LAPWING
    Carton of eggs
COULTER
    BRANDISH's suit with notebook in
        jacket

BRANDISH
    Sack

Offstage R:
VICKIE
    Nightdress
SANDRA
    Phial of liquid

ACT THREE
Contract and cheque book in table
    drawer

Offstage L:
HAZEL
    Two cups of tea
    Bowl of porridge and spoon
    Cup of tea
    Swimsuit and towel
    Letter
KENTON
    Cup of tea
    Ball-point pen
LAPWING
    Milk can
    Large blue pencil
    Enormous pencil
COULTER
    Slice of toast
VICKIE
    Suitcase

PERSONAL
KENTON
    Sheets of typescript, notebook,
        agreement
VICKIE
    Suitcase, photograph of SANDRA
COULTER
    Briefcase containing encyclopaedia
        material and contract, ball-point
        pen
BRANDISH
    Card, pen

COSTUME PLOT

KENTON
Casually dressed in slacks, sports shirt, cardigan, etc.
VICKIE
Summer two-piece suit (Acts I and II)
Cotton dress (Act III)
SANDRA
Jumper suit (Act I)
Summer dress (Acts II and III)
COULTER
Rather shabby suit

DA SILVA
Very well cut suit (Act I)
Vividly coloured leisure shirt and slacks (Acts II and III)
HAZEL
Cotton shirt, jeans and sneakers
LAPWING
Cord trousers, shabby tweed jacket and battered felt hat
BRANDISH
Sober business suit
Sack (End of Act II)